THE INTERNET BUSINESS PRIMER

Wayne Allison

Copyright © 1996 by Wayne Allison
Cover design © 1996 by Sourcebooks, Inc.

All rights reserved. No part of this book may be reproduced in any form or by any electronic or mechanical means including information storage and retrieval systems—except in the case of brief quotations embodied in critical articles or reviews, or in the case of the exercises in this book solely for the personal use of the purchaser—without permission in writing from its publisher, Sourcebooks, Inc.

Trademarks: All brand names and product names used in this book are trademarks, registered trademarks, or trade names of their respective holders. Sourcebooks, Inc. is not associated with any product or vendor in this book.

Published by: **Sourcebooks, Inc.**
P.O. Box 372, Naperville, Illinois, 60566
(708) 961-3900
FAX: 708-961-2168

Editorial: Todd Stocke
Cover Design: Wayne Johnson/Dominique Raccah
Interior Design and Production: Wayne Johnson, Sourcebooks, Inc.

This publication is designed to provide accurate and authoritative information in regard to the subject matter covered. It is sold with the understanding that the publisher is not engaged in rendering legal, accounting, or other professional service. If legal advice or other expert assistance is required, the services of a competent professional person should be sought.
*From a Declaration of Principles Jointly Adopted by a Committee of the
American Bar Association and a Committee of Publishers and Associations*

The **Small Business Sourcebooks** series is designed to help you teach yourself the business essentials you need to be successful. All books in the series are available for bulk sales. Call us for information or a catalog. Other books in the series include:

- *Mancuso's Small Business Resource Guide*
- *The Small Business Legal Guide*
- *Great Idea! Now What?*
- *How to Market Your Business*
- *Real World Customer Service*
- *Your First Business Plan*
- *Getting Paid in Full*
- *Smart Hiring*
- *The Small Business Start-Up Guide*
- *How to Get a Loan or Line of Credit*

Library of Congress Cataloging-in-Publication Data
Allison, Wayne
    The Internet business primer / Wayne Allison.
       p. cm. — (Small business sourcebooks)
    ISBN 1-57071-064-3 (pbk.)
    1. Internet (Computer network) 2. Industrial management—Communication systems. 3. Business enterprises—Communication systems. 4. Information technology—Management. I. Title II. Series.
HD30.37.A38   1996
025.06'65 — dc20

95-52112
CIP

Printed and bound in the United States of America.
Paperback — 10 9 8 7 6 5 4 3 2 1

Table of Contents

Acknowledgements v
Preface vii
Introduction 1
Chapter 1: Introduction to the Internet 5
Chapter 2: Business on the Internet 11
Chapter 3: Assessing Your Business 19
Chapter 4: Business Operations 29
Chapter 5: Customers 31
Chapter 6: Products 39
Chapter 7: Marketing 43
Chapter 8: Sales 53
Chapter 9: Suppliers. 57
Chapter 10: International 59
Chapter 11: Technical 61
Chapter 12: Your Competitors 69
Chapter 13: Security 71

Chapter 14: Making the Decisions 77
Appendix Contents 79
Appendix A: Hardware Alternatives 81
Appendix B: Software Alternatives 85
Appendix C: Communications Alternatives 91
Appendix D: Service Provider Alternatives 95
Appendix E: Questions for Internet Service Providers . 99
Appendix F: More Detailed Analysis 105
Appendix G: An Example 107
Glossary: 111

Acknowledgements

My great appreciation to my family for their support in the creation of this book: my wife, Julie, as chief editor, reviewer, time allocation manager, and primarily responsible for promoting the effort behind this book; my two year old son, Jake (a.k.a. Rufus), for not destroying too much of the materials during their creation; my parents, Pat and Ira, who subtly nudged and convinced me to use my brain in spite of my knowledge that they didn't know what they were talking about.

Preface

As a business manager, the consistent objective in all of your responsibilities is to increase profitable revenues while minimizing expense. With that in mind, as the president of a small technology import distributor, I felt the media and industry pressure to "be on the Internet," so I began gathering information.

When trying to educate myself on the subject, I quickly found that despite the claims that the Internet is where fortunes are made and businesses of all kinds will find success, I could very easily spend thousands of dollars and hundreds of hours just trying to determine what to actually do to "be on the Internet."

The Internet Business Primer came about as a result of an observation of:

 The seemingly hysterical media hype of the "Information Superhighway" (i.e., Internet).

 The overwhelming number of sources of information regarding the Internet.

 The wide variance in content of information being published to describe the Internet.

Preface

📖 The apparent gap in information available to the average business person wanting to find out about the Internet.

In the end, I determined that there is one primary question to ask yourself as a business manager when exploring the possible use of the Internet:

"At this time, for my business, is it worth it to be on the Internet at all?"

This guide will help you to clearly answer this question from a business perspective. Answering this question incorrectly can be costly.

There are two possible answers to this question:

NO

In which case, after reading this guide, you will know why not, and what to look for over time to indicate that the answer should be YES.

YES

In which case, after reading this guide, you will have two valuable pieces of information:

1. What being "on the Internet" means.

2. How to best apply and utilize the Internet for business purposes.

This guide is the result of hundreds of hours of research into the Internet from a business manager's perspective. This guide outlines not only what the Internet is and what can be done there, but most importantly, it will assist you in assessing business benefits you can/cannot, should/should not be working to realize on the Internet.

Introduction to the Guide

Objective

The only thing in the U.S. today that appears to get more hype than the Internet is the Super Bowl. Super Bowl commercials cost in the $1 million range per 30 seconds. They are potentially seen by millions of viewers, and then they're over. In order to show those millions of viewers more information, you must belly-up to the bar with another $1 million. That's how it works, and it can be very effective marketing.

The Internet is receiving hype that not only rivals that of the Super Bowl, but is growing at astronomical rates. You can't reach hundreds of millions of viewers in a 30 second period, but it doesn't cost $1 million either. You can, however, potentially reach tens of millions of viewers, and you're not limited to 30 second slots.

Sound interesting? It certainly does, as evidenced by the rush of newcomers to the Internet—both individuals and businesses. However, the Internet is still somewhat bewildering, and to compound matters, it lends itself to being hyped by throwing around the type of numbers we have here.

Introduction to the Guide

It is difficult to ignore the noise being created about the Internet, but a huge gray area exists in the minds of many business people. There are some fundamental questions being asked daily by thousands of people. Questions such as:

- What is the Internet?

- Who is really using it?

- What does all this techno-mumble-jumble mean?

- What if I want to learn more? Who do I talk to?

- What kind of "service" do all of these "Internet Service Providers" offer?

- How much of the hype should I believe?

- Why am I being led to worry that I am not already "on the Internet"?

- Are my competitors really "on it"?

- Are my customers really "on it"?

And the bottom line question of all questions:

- How can I incrementally increase my business by being on the Internet?

Unfortunately, the typical answers to these questions have a number of consistent components:

1. They get technical very quickly.

2. There seem to be real costs involved, without clear benefits.

3. They all are relatively generic and full of assumptions.

Introduction to the Guide

This guide is designed to:

1. Provide a non-technical business perspective of the Internet to a business person.

2. Outline the specific business options available for consideration.

3. Outline the possible costs and benefits involved.

Who Should Read This Guide?

Business Managers, Presidents, Executives, Business Owners— Anyone who has the responsibility of operating a business.

There are literally hundreds, if not over a thousand, books, video tapes, audio tapes, and seminars being hyper-hyped as the definitive source of information on the Internet. By and large, all of them are very good at communicating information at a certain level. In fact, after completing **The Internet Business Primer**, you will have, at least, a clear idea of what you want to know more about and will be much better prepared to select the source that will give you the information you need.

You may already have some idea of what the Internet is. Your concept may be right, wrong, or somewhere in the middle. Regardless, this guide will help you understand what it really is, and more importantly, how to best put it to business use.

What This Guide Is Not

The Internet provides a wide variety of discussion points, each of which can be analyzed to virtually limitless degrees. Since the Clinton Administration jumped on the Internet bandwagon by promoting the Information Superhighway and providing additional federal funding, the ongoing discussions have grown to almost nauseating proportions.

Introduction to the Guide

With that being said, this guide is not:

- A technology document.

- A Marketing-Hype document.

- A Get-Rich-Quick scheme.

- A history book on the Internet.

- Another exploitation in the current hype-circus surrounding the Internet.

There are plenty of all of the above available from just about any bookstore or computer store. They are typically accompanied by a variety of claims that support the frenzy of the Internet. These claims range from the get-rich-quick variety to the FUD angle (Fear, Uncertainty, Doubt), prompting you to believe that if you do not get on the Internet today, your business will most certainly die within the year.

The Internet Business Primer is none of these things.

What You Can Expect

Every business is different, and as such, application of the Internet to any given business is different.

After reading **The Internet Business Primer**, you will:

1. Have a clear picture of what the Internet is and is not.

2. Have specific, concrete business options as to what you can, cannot, should and should not do on the Internet, including separation of the hype benefits from the true pros and cons as they relate to your business.

3. Be able to determine a business-oriented cost justification for using (or choosing not to use) the Internet.

Chapter One

Introduction to the Internet

What Is The Internet?

A General Definition

The Internet, or Information Superhighway as it has been termed, is quite simply a collection of publicly accessible computers, all tied together on a publicly accessible network. There are two primary components to what we call the Internet:

Computers. Thousands upon thousands of computers worldwide that are connected 24 hours a day, seven days a week. Each is accessible by anyone with an Internet ID, and each provides some type of information or service.

People. Millions of individuals worldwide who, at any given time of day or night, are "on the 'Net" doing work, sending electronic mail, "talking" to other people, wasting time, or exploring any one of the thousands upon thousands of computers and information sources out there in the world.

Introduction to the Internet

As of the beginning of 1995, the Internet was estimated to have over 250,000 separate destinations. A destination is a point on the Internet that holds specific information which is separate and apart from all the other points of information. It could be a single file of information, a program, a computer dedicated to a specific topic, or even a complete catalog and ordering facility for a particular company's product line. This number is growing at well over 6,000 destinations per month.

History

The Internet is over 20 years old and was originally (and still is to a great extent) a research and development tool for engineers and scientists. It was funded primarily by the government (National Science Foundation, under Research & Development grants) to facilitate the exchange of information, research, analysis, tools, and hundreds of other scientific/technical informational packages (software, white papers, research papers, etc.).

Additionally, the Internet provided a means whereby all of these technical folks could communicate with one another relatively inexpensively. Electronic mail, on-line "chatting," and discussion groups fostered an ongoing, little-known world of technical communications.

This resulted in a network of computers managed by highly technical people for highly technical people. Obviously, it was not the type of thing that the average business was utilizing.

Today

Recently, however, the Internet has been discovered by the masses. So much so that the original funding agency, the National Science Foundation (NSF), created an "Acceptable Use Policy" to discourage non-NSF "sanctioned" activities on the network (i.e., business and/or entertainment use).

There are a number of reasons for the recent Internet discovery by the masses. However, the important point is not how the Internet became known and promoted outside the technical community,

but rather the fact that it is now very much known and promoted in the business community. Total Internet business in 1994 was estimated to be in the $100-200 million range, which was primarily comprised of the service and software providers, not business-to-business electronic commerce. In a country where overall business is measured in the billions and trillions, this amount of commerce doesn't even represent a drop in the bucket. This fact, however, is poised to change, and change quickly.

As it has evolved, the Internet has gotten considerably easier to use than in its infancy. It can now be accessed by any type of computer (PC, Macintosh, Unix, etc.), and is now providing access methods that incorporate text, graphics, sound, and even pictures with motion.

There is also no shortage of companies out there offering all the things you need to be on the Internet. The Internet offers some real business opportunities today. However, without a business-oriented plan, it is all too easy for the average business person to be sucked in by the hype and end up wasting money, time, and resources.

The fact of the matter is that the companies making the most money on the Internet are those hyping the Internet, not those actually selling their goods and services on the Internet. This, however, is changing.

Today, a clear business perspective of the Internet is essential before rushing out to the computer store to buy software, or calling a service provider to have him milk your company for services you don't need.

The Future

The exact future of the Internet is, like most technology, somewhat unknown. There are, however, a number of points to be aware of before writing the Internet off as a technology fad.

People. There are already tens of millions of users world-

Introduction to the Internet

wide. There are now estimates of 30-60 million Internet users (i.e., individuals who connect to the Internet from time to time and for one reason or another). To put this in perspective, the combined membership of the three most popular on-line service providers (CompuServe, Prodigy, America On-Line) is less than 10 million. That means that the Internet represents a new medium to potentially reach these people with a message. Just like any other medium, it may or may not be an effective way for your business to communicate (e.g., a one million dollar per minute Super Bowl ad will reach millions of viewers, but advertising food additive compounds will probably not help sell more of them).

Information. The categories of information available on the Internet are too exhaustive to try to keep up with. The news groups, discussion groups, and general information exchanges that take place on the 'Net are limited only by the millions of users' imaginations. Topics ranging from business finance to pornography can be readily found, along with as much or as little detailed information as anyone could want.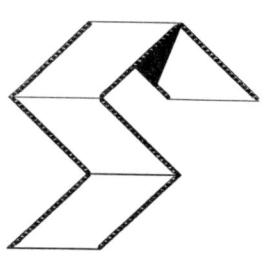

The Network Itself. The Internet, today, is being used 99.99% of the time for text and graphics applications. It is important to note, however, that the Internet can technically support not only text and graphics, but voice and video as well.

Growth Rate. The Internet population of users is growing at a rate that will at least double in 1996. The number of businesses using the Internet is growing at twice the rate of the Internet itself. Projections estimate that by the year 2000, business-to-business electronic commerce will be $50 billion annually.

Big Players. There are a number of major corporations making themselves known on the Internet in a variety of ways. The company that will most likely have the most

Introduction to the Internet

influence in the near term is Microsoft. Microsoft's release of the much-awaited next version of its popular Windows package (termed Windows 95) comes with Internet access built in. Right out of the box, Windows 95 allows a user to access the Internet in order to get to Microsoft corporation electronically for support. If Windows 95 has anywhere near the impact and acceptance that Windows has had in the past, then you can expect an additional 30 million or so users to be connected to the Internet by the end of 1996.

Will you and/or your business be using the Internet? The odds are high that you will. The question is, how will you use it, and when and how will it actually pay off?

Who Owns The Internet?

No one actually "owns" the Internet. Unlike on-line computer services such as CompuServe, Prodigy, or America On-Line, there is not a company called "Internet Corporation" that owns the Internet.

Remember that the Internet is a collection of computers and users. Each computer is owned by someone, and that person or business is responsible for maintaining it and its connection into the network itself.

Each Internet user is responsible for his or her own use of the Internet. Network etiquette, or "netiquette" as it has been termed, is something that Internet users are quite familiar with. For example, a user who signs on and then sends an electronic mail promoting his or her product to everyone in every discussion group available can get "flamed." The term "flame" is used to describe what happens when millions of Internet users get upset at someone who violates netiquette. Many times, users decide to send the violator electronic mail expressing their anger at the same time, which usually results in computers crashing, many nasty phone calls, and possible service revocation.

Introduction to the Internet

The Internet is owned by no one, and everyone. The users themselves comprise the Internet and have the most influence over its direction and appropriate usage. This is clearly a very open and dynamic arena for information exchange. Given the fact that so many businesses are trying to take advantage of the Internet, they will inevitably have a huge impact on how business is conducted there.

There are committees comprised of volunteers that regularly review the Internet from a variety of perspectives, mostly technical. These groups outline and publish standards that are by and large adhered to worldwide. However, these groups are primarily focused on the technology and technical advancement of the Internet itself. What they do is very important to the average Internet user. However, it typically does not directly affect any particular user's actual work or interaction with the Internet.

Chapter Two

Business on the Internet

Should You Be "On The 'Net"?

There is a lot of noise in the world right now proclaiming and promoting "business on the Internet." If you make a giant leap and assume that your business should definitely be on the Internet, what exactly does that mean?

◈ Should you rush out and guess which software package to buy at the local computer store?

◈ Should you respond to one of the dozens of mailings you've been getting regarding an Internet seminar?

◈ Should you call one of the Internet Service Providers that are advertising so heavily these days?

◈ Should you buy computer hardware to connect to the Internet?

◈ Should you ask one of your key technical employees to get you on the Internet?

The answer to the question "should my business be on the Internet?" might very well be "yes." This is the easy question. The harder questions are: "to what degree?" "for what business purposes?" and, "how will it benefit my business?" Once you answer these questions, there are hundreds of books, software packages, system integrators, service providers, and value-added resellers that can tell you how and/or help you actually get on the Internet—for a fee.

There are plenty of reasons why the Internet is growing so quickly, and those are the same reasons that you should probably be on the Internet. However, this is not to say that you should be doing *business* on the Internet. The Internet is, at minimum, a place to educate yourself, ask questions, get answers, and be entertained. All of this is good, and when used properly, can be worth the costs. However, this level of usage is a far cry from actually conducting a component of your business on the Internet.

What Business Uses Are On The Internet?

There are many possible business uses of the Internet. Capitalizing on the Internet from a business perspective is only in its infancy. The rate of increase in business use is astounding. However, the rate of success is another matter that the jury has yet to determine. The jury is the average consumer. Will the average consumer buy clothing, pizzas,  appliances, automobiles, books, stock quotes, or anything else electronically? Or will he or she continue to go to the mall, pick up the phone, or use a mail order catalog?

If you look at the number and size of the companies that are spending millions to gain a presence on the Internet, then you would have to conclude that the Internet is a sure bet for business. Maybe. Maybe not.

As for what is available today for the average business, that is what this guide is all about.

An effective manner of conceptualizing the business uses of the Internet is to break out the Internet Applications from the Business Applications. Keep in mind that the Applications available on the Internet are not limited to a one-way transaction (like an advertisement in a magazine, for example). The Internet provides for two-way communication whenever and wherever a business would want to make it available.

Internet Applications

The term "Internet Applications," as used here, is meant to describe the "things you can do" on the Internet. Specifically, some of the most utilized and effective Internet Applications used by businesses today are:

- Electronic Mail—E-Mail (the most utilized Internet application).
- Document Management and Distribution.
- Software Distribution.
- Forms Management and Distribution.
- Information/Knowledge Advancement.
- Product Catalog Management and Distribution.
- Product Ordering Mechanisms.
- Product Delivery Mechanisms.
- Research and Development Advancement.

Business Applications

The term "Business Applications" as used here, is meant to describe the business things you can do on the Internet. There are a variety of profitable, intelligent Business Applications available today, including:

Internal Business Communications: Efficient, cost-effective communications between employees, departments, office locations, etc.

External Business Communications: Efficient, cost-effective communications to and from your customers, prospects, suppliers, and any other entity with which your business exchanges information.

Technical: Information on virtually any subject, product, industry, or topic of the day can be found on the Internet. This is especially true of technology topics. Engineers, scientists, research, design, and development personnel are some of the fastest to realize tangible benefits from Internet access.

Marketing — Input: Marketing departments are always looking for a better way to identify prospects and keep ahead of competitors. The Internet offers a vast treasure of product, industry, and marketing research, much of which comes directly from customers.

Marketing — Output: Marketing departments are quickly recognizing that any medium that provides potential exposure to millions of people around the clock is something to explore. The ability to post product information and announcements, communicate with the press, and solicit feedback from customers and prospects is a welcomed marketing tool.

Catalogs: Businesses that produce catalogs of their products may be able to quickly cost justify putting their catalog on the Internet. Any publication produced for internal or external use is a prospect for publishing on-line. End-users of the catalog can browse, search, print, or save the information at any time. The current production expenses can be decreased while increasing consumer access to the catalog.

Product Delivery: For businesses that offer "soft" products (e.g., services, information, data, software, etc.), the Internet offers a unique vehicle to actually deliver these products electronically to end-users.

Product Introductions: Again for companies that offer "soft" products, the Internet offers a vehicle that allows a customer to try-before-they-buy. Many businesses are putting "abbreviated" versions of their software and/or informational services on the Internet in order to let prospects evaluate them before they purchase a complete version.

Ordering: For businesses that sell material goods (i.e., not "soft" products), or for companies that are uncomfortable sending their products out electronically, one thing always has to be done—an order must be placed, accepted, and acknowledged. On-line ordering is yet another Business Application that is being rapidly put to use on the Internet by companies selling virtually all types of products.

Information Gathering: The Internet offers specific discussion groups, news groups, and publications that are open to everyone. There are specific discussion groups on virtually every industry and niche in the marketplace. Beyond that, these interactive groups further specialize in individual product types. For example, there are not simply discussion groups in place to facilitate talk about computers, but literally hundreds of separate groups that talk about specific topics relating to computers (e.g., comp.ibm.pc.games.flt-sim is the name of a group that is in place for anyone who wishes to talk, ask and/or answer questions about Flight Simulator Games made for IBM Personal Computers).

Government: There are thousands of companies that do business with the government. Many of these companies subscribe and regularly read the Commerce Business Daily, a publication that lists all government bids, requests, etc. This publication is available via the Internet. Also, companies that interact with the government or are somehow tied to government action will find that many arms of the government are already on the Internet (e.g., you can send mail to the President at the Internet address President@WHITEHOUSE.GOV).

Publications: At the time this guide was created, the number of magazines, trade journals, and publications on the Internet numbered in the hundreds. The astonishing thing is that they are being put on the Internet at a rate that is difficult to keep up with. A particularly nice feature of many publications on the Internet is that the publishers typically implement a search and cross-reference feature that allows a user to call up, for example, all articles in the past X months that mention a specific phrase. (If the average business manager is at all like myself, there are plenty of stacks of old magazines lying around "just in case I need to refer to that.")

Authors: If your company in any way authors documents (i.e., books, novels, documentation, etc.), you will find that your colleagues are quickly exploiting the Internet in many ways. These ways range from general discussions, to publication reviews, to actual publishing on the Internet.

The above Business Applications are categorized relatively generally and do not tell you what is cost justifiable. However, these categories should give you a flavor of what is possible.

Many business managers see a list such as the one above and immediately jump into the Internet. Perhaps it is a mistake, perhaps it is not. If you do jump onto the Internet, you will certainly gain experience in what is there and what you could do. You will also spend a lot of time and money trying to figure out what you should do, and how you should go about it.

"Presence" On The Internet

Before attempting to determine what are the proper Internet Applications to employ for your Business Applications, it is helpful to define what "presence" on the Internet is.

If someone hands you a business card with an Internet address on it (e.g., fbuehuler@asystem.com), that means they are on the Internet, right? The answer is a qualified yes. This minimally means that this person is accessible via Internet mail. This could additionally mean a number of other things. For example, the company that this person works for may have individual Internet mail addresses for each employee. This person may have his or her own Internet address through an Internet service provider because he or she benefits from the additional method of communicating. Perhaps this company has their own computer hardware system(s) set up specifically for, and dedicated to, the Internet.

In any case, this person has presence on the Internet. As for a business itself, a presence on the Internet can mean a wide variety of things, all entailing various costs and benefits (or potential benefits).

The range of Internet presence is essentially what this book is all about. Determining to what level your business should be on the Internet is the trick. You should also clearly understand that the general Internet confusion that now exists is being exploited by hundreds of vendors marketing for your attention. Not only do you have to determine what level of Internet presence is right for your company, but you also must have enough knowledge to make sure you don't get robbed when trying to get connected.

For example, in the business card scenario described above, if the person had an individual Internet address, he could be paying a flat monthly fee of $15, $20, $100, or more. He may or may not be paying an hourly access fee which goes straight to his monthly credit card bill. The primary difference is the cost! Whether he is paying $20 or $200 per month, his usage is the same. (See Appendix G, An Example, for a real description of how my company learned this lesson the hard way.)

The following graphic provides an overview of the primary business uses of the Internet and their relative degree of difficulty in implementation. Note that the degree of difficulty can involve not only use of resources within your company, but outside services as well (for a fee).

All of the above constitute a presence on the Internet and are

Low Presence   **High Presence**

Degree of Difficulty to Implement

Application
- E-Mail (personal or company)
- Individual Internet Browsing & News Groups
- Textual Home Page
- Graphical Home Page
- Interactive Home Page
- Order Processing
- Order Fulfillment

cumulative. For example, if you want to have a graphical Home Page, then you will implicitly have e-mail and Internet browsing.

It is not too difficult to see why the whole subject, when discussed beyond the conceptual level in order to determine a company action, can be confusing. Consider the following:

✐ Each level of presence entails additional costs.

✐ The real value of each level of service is difficult to gauge due to the newness of business on the Internet.

✐ There are a wide variety of ways to implement each level of presence.

✐ There are no wrong ways of implementing any level of presence. There are only pros and cons in reference to what the business objectives are.

✐ The service providers, software, hardware, and communications choices available today are:

    1. Numerous (to say the least).
    2. Inconsistent in pricing (there are Info-Highway bandits out there making money on market ignorance now!).

The next chapter will guide you through an analysis of your business that will help you get started by forcing you to think and document what you do today, how you do it, and how it can be *effectively* improved with the Internet. The key word here is "*effectively*," in that improvement can be made to just about any component of a business. However, the questions that you must keep in mind are "at what cost?" and "what are the business benefits?"

Chapter Three

Assessing *Your* Business

As with most other things on our planet with moderate to high complexity, a business is comprised of various components. From the smallest to the largest business, each has similar functions, features, and objectives.

Given that we are discussing business, there is an assumption being made that says your business is doing something in an effort to make money. That something could be a service, a product that you design and/or manufacture, or possibly a product that you buy and in turn resell. It really doesn't matter which, because your business, like all others, is doing what it is doing to make money. The trick is to do it in such a way that you don't spend more than you make in the process.

The components of an operation, regardless of size, that is operating as a business are generally categorized as follows for the next few chapters of business assessment:

- ◎ General Business

- ◎ Business Operations

- ◎ Customers

Assessing Your Business

- Products
- Marketing
- Sales
- Suppliers
- International
- Technical

In the following chapters, each of the above business component categories is discussed in reference to possible business uses on the Internet. The objective of these chapters is to guide you through a thought process in reviewing what your business does, how it does it, and if using the Internet could be beneficial.

General Business

The general industry that your business is in is an important component of your analysis. Discussion groups alone can be enough of a justification to use the Internet. Depending on your type of business and what vertical industry you are in, you may find an invaluable source of ongoing information in one or more on-line discussion groups.

The Internet offers a wide variety of special interest groups, many of which are categorized by industry and/or interest type. For example, the following table outlines only a few of those available on a discussion group system (called a "News Server"). In fact, in late 1995, when this information was pulled from only one of many News Servers available on the Internet, there were over 7,000 individual discussion groups. Try to ignore the strange wording and punctuation in the discussion group name. This is the way in which the News Servers categorize related (or semi-related) topics.

Assessing Your Business

On-Line Discussion Groups

Industry and/or Interest	Discussion/News Group Name
Agriculture	alt.sustainable.agriculture clari.biz.industry.agriculture fedreg.agriculture sci.agriculture sci.agriculture.beekeeping
Authoring / Publishing	bit.listserv.authorware comp.publish.prepress relcom.commerce.publishing biz.books.technical
Banking / Finance	clari.biz.finance clari.biz.finance.personal clari.biz.finance.services fedreg.finance ucb.financial-aid.info clari.biz.industry.banking relcom.banktech
Broadcasting / Media	alt.news-media ba.broadcast chi.media clari.biz.industry.broadcasting clari.biz.industry.print_media clari.tw.new_media git.media-talk rec.radio.broadcasting uk.media
Construction	clari.biz.industry.construction pdaxs.jobs.construction relcom.commerce.construction slac.building-mgr ucb.building-coord
Education	alt.education.disabled clari.news.education clari.news.education.higher

Assessing Your Business

clari.tw.education
fedreg.education
misc.education
misc.education.adult
misc.education.language.english
pdaxs.issues.education

Employment

biz.jobs.offered
ba.jobs.contract
ba.jobs.misc
ba.jobs.offered
biz.jobs.offered
dod.jobs
git.ohr.jobs.digest
misc.jobs.contract
misc.jobs.offered
misc.jobs.offered.entry
misc.jobs.resumes
pdaxs.jobs.clerical
pdaxs.jobs.computers
pdaxs.jobs.construction
pdaxs.jobs.engineering
pdaxs.jobs.management
pdaxs.jobs.resumes
pdaxs.jobs.retail
pdaxs.jobs.wanted
relcom.commerce.jobs
vmsnet.employment

Energy

clari.biz.industry.energy
fedreg.energy
relcom.commerce.energy
sci.energy
sci.energy.hydrogen

Food

clari.biz.industry.food
pdaxs.ads.food
rec.food.recipes
rec.food.restaurants
relcom.commerce.food
relcom.commerce.food.drinks
relcom.commerce.food.sweet

Assessing Your Business

Foreign Interest	clari.canada.biz
	clari.biz.market.report.asia
	clari.biz.market.report.europe
	clari.news.canada
	clari.news.europe
	clari.news.usa.gov.foreign_policy
	clari.world.americas.canada.business
	clari.world.asia
General Business	alt.business.misc
	alt.business.multi-level
	biz.misc
	clari.biz.briefs
	clari.biz.commodity
	clari.biz.courts
	clari.biz.earnings
	clari.biz.economy
	clari.biz.economy.world
	clari.biz.finance
	clari.biz.finance.earnings
	clari.biz.finance.personal
Government	fedreg.govern
	alt.politics.democrats.governors
	bit.listserv.govdoc-l
	ca.govt-bulletins
	clari.news.gov
	clari.news.gov.officials
	clari.news.gov.state
	clari.news.gov.taxes
	clari.news.usa.gov.white_house
	courts.usa.federal.supreme
Health / Medical	clari.biz.industry.health
	clari.tw.health
	clari.tw.health.aids
	fedreg.health
	misc.health.alternative
	misc.health.diabetes
	relcom.commerce.medicine

Assessing Your Business

	sci.med.telemedicine
	talk.politics.medicine
	ucb.school-pub-health
Insurance	clari.biz.industry.insurance
	pdaxs.services.insurance
Legal	alt.law-enforcement
	bit.listserv.lawsch-l
	clari.biz.courts
	clari.news.law
	clari.news.law.civil
	clari.news.law.crime
	clari.news.law.profession
	clari.news.usa.law
	courts.usa.config
	courts.usa.federal.supreme
	fedreg.legal
	misc.legal
	pdaxs.services.legal
Manufacturing	clari.biz.industry.manufacturing
	sci.engr.manufacturing
Politics	ab.politics
	alt.politics.datahighway
	alt.politics.economics
	alt.politics.elections
	alt.politics.libertarian
	alt.politics.perot
	alt.politics.usa.constitution
	alt.politics.democrats
	alt.politics.usa.republican
	clari.news.politics
	clari.news.usa.gov.politics
Retail	clari.biz.industry.retail
	pdaxs.jobs.retail
Services Industry	clari.biz.finance.services
	clari.biz.industry.services

Assessing Your Business

misc.emerg-services
mn.online-service
pdaxs.ads.cars.service
pdaxs.services.accounting
pdaxs.services.appliance
pdaxs.services.carpentry
pdaxs.services.children
pdaxs.services.cleaning
pdaxs.services.computers
pdaxs.services.consulting
pdaxs.services.counseling
pdaxs.services.electrical
pdaxs.services.financial
pdaxs.services.fitness
pdaxs.services.gardening
pdaxs.services.graphics
pdaxs.services.insurance
pdaxs.services.int_design
pdaxs.services.landscaping
pdaxs.services.legal
pdaxs.services.massage
pdaxs.services.misc
pdaxs.services.moving
pdaxs.services.music
pdaxs.services.painting
pdaxs.services.pets
pdaxs.services.photo
pdaxs.services.plumbing
pdaxs.services.roofing
pdaxs.services.security
pdaxs.services.storage
pdaxs.services.wordproc

Stock Market

clari.biz.market.otc
clari.biz.market.report.usa.nyse
clari.tw.stocks
info.nysersnmp
misc.invest.stocks
ny.nysernet
ny.nysernet.map
ny.nysernet.maps

Assessing Your Business

	ny.nysernet.nic
	ny.nysernet.nysertech
	relcom.commerce.stocks
Taxes	clari.news.gov.taxes
	misc.taxes
Tourism	clari.biz.industry.tourism
Transportation	alt.autos.antique
	alt.autos.camaro.firebird
	alt.autos.rod-n-custom
	alt.cad.autocad
	alt.snowmobiles
	aus.aviation
	ba.transportation
	bit.listserv.autocat
	bit.listserv.nettrain
	clari.biz.industry.automotive
	clari.biz.industry.aviation
	clari.biz.industry.transportation
	clari.news.aviation
	fedreg.transport
	nj.market.autos
	rec.autos.antique
	rec.autos.driving
	rec.autos.marketplace
	rec.autos.misc
	rec.autos.rod-n-custom
	rec.autos.simulators
	rec.autos.sport
	rec.autos.sport.info
	rec.autos.sport.nascar
	rec.autos.sport.tech
	rec.autos.tech
	rec.autos.vw
	rec.aviation.announce
	rec.aviation.answers
	rec.aviation.homebuilt
	rec.aviation.ifr
	rec.aviation.military

Assessing Your Business

```
rec.aviation.misc
rec.aviation.owning
rec.aviation.piloting
rec.aviation.products
rec.aviation.questions
rec.aviation.simulators
rec.aviation.student
relcom.commerce.transport
tnn.internet.mobile
triangle.transport
```

The reason that these group names appear so esoteric is that they are grouped into categories so that there is some order. For example, some of the prefixes used have meanings such as:

Prefix	**Meaning / Grouping**
alt	Alternative related (catch-all category)
biz	Business related
comp	Computer related
misc	Miscellaneous
rec	Recreation
sci	Science related

These discussion groups are there for interested users to read, comment, ask questions, get answers, etc.

If, for example, you are involved in the food industry, then you might find out what some of your customers, competitors, or other interested parties are discussing (possibly about your products) in the group 'clari.biz.industry.food'. Another example that exemplifies the degree of granularity you can find is the group called 'rec.music.a-cappella', devoted to the discussion of acappella music.

Assessing Your Business

These groups are extremely dynamic, and can have literally thousands of conversations going on at any time. There are two pieces of good news regarding this as an application for business:

1. If there are groups that are aligned with your business interests, then you will most likely learn more than you can imagine by simply reading the comments that are posted daily.

2. The fact that there are thousands of groups means that there is something for anyone and everyone.

As you might be wondering, a list of thousands of anything can be cumbersome. Fortunately the Internet software makes traversing, sorting, viewing, and general use of these groups quite easy, even for a novice computer user.

The deepest pool of information on the Internet, by industry, is in the "technical" world. This includes virtually all forms of "technology," from computers to aerospace to biology to chemistry to physics to you-name-it. This is not to say that there is not much non-technical information on the Internet, but there is perhaps less depth of information in these areas. However, this will not be the case for long. The most astonishing Internet growth rate is coming from the non-technical community, primarily businesses and average consumers.

Chapter Four

Business Operations

Business operations is a general term that must be further broken down when assessing possible areas for Internet usage. The most utilized and easiest form of Internet usage for business is in the area of communications. Communications, both internal and external, is an area that the Internet can offer a real cost justification for your business.

For example, if your business has a remote office, field personnel, or in any way has a need to communicate internally, then the Internet offers electronic mail facilities that are easy and powerful. Sample communication-oriented Business Applications range from simple e-mail to questionnaires, announcements, policy updates, and schedules.

Thousands of businesses have remote offices or locations where employees or agents work from their homes. Many of these businesses have built internal communications facilities that allow them to send e-mail, documents, schedules, and generally communicate electronically. These are internal-use networks that the company installs, pays for, and maintains.

Why pay for the network? The Internet is everywhere and can be accessed with a simple phone line. The Internet offers an ideal vehicle for internal communications.

Chapter Five

Customers

In order to justify the cost of putting your business on the Internet, you must make a complete assessment of your customers. This cost justification assessment involves asking yourself a number of questions.

How do you communicate with your customers?

In Person? The Internet certainly cannot take the place of a face-to-face sales call. However, if some portion of your sales calls involves simply dropping off or picking up information (i.e., not products or physical goods), then the Internet could provide you with a more effective method of delivering or receiving this information.

Phone? If you find that your employees play a lot of phone tag with your customers just to give information, ask questions, or get input or feedback, then the Internet offers a less intrusive, more efficient manner of communicating.

Fax? The fax machine is a wonderful invention, but it has some drawbacks that can be supplanted with Internet usage. As more and more information (forms, documents, etc.) is created and managed with computers, the distribution of these documents can be done effectively with the Internet.

The real problem with faxing that is overcome through the Internet is similar to the phone tag game. If the person you are trying to fax doesn't pick up the fax or is out of town, for example, will they get the fax? When? Anything that can be faxed can also be sent electronically over the Internet. The receiver of the information can read it, print it, modify it, respond to it, and/or send it back.

Mail/Overnight Delivery? Again, like the fax method, virtually any document sent via mail or overnight delivery can be sent via the Internet. The Internet not only offers cost savings over mail/overnight, it also provides delivery service directly to the recipient's desk almost immediately (certainly quicker than mail or overnight).

Newsletters? A tried and true method of enhancing customer relations is the company newsletter. A company newsletter offers a medium of communication that informs customers of recent changes in your company, product announcements, promotions and enhancements, and generally keeps your company in the minds of customers. Newsletters are a wonderful idea for many companies, but they do entail costs and resource consumption. Posting company newsletters on the Internet has a number of benefits:

✓ Customers can always get to the information.

✓ They don't lose it.

✓ They can print it only if they want to.

✓ They can respond directly to your company.

✓ They can easily clip, save, and/or distribute information that they feel is important to their business.

✓ The costs are typically less than those of a hard copy publication.

What do you communicate to your customers?

Typical business communications to customers include:

* Notifications.

* Product and service updates.

* Product and service announcements.

* Price changes.

* Thank you letters.

* Order status.

Any and all of the above communications are prospects for Internet communication. Distributing them on the Internet may enhance your business through increased efficiency and decreased costs.

How and what do your customers communicate to you?

Typical business communications from customers include:

◆ Order status requests.

◆ Product feedback.

◆ Support questions.

◆ Process requests (e.g., orders, credit requests, etc.).

◆ Marketing response (e.g., "bingo" cards, fax-back, etc.).

◆ Complaints.

◆ Letters of appreciation.

Customers

The above list is certainly not exhaustive. However, it is fairly representative of the typical types of customer communications. They can come in a variety of forms, including all of the forms your business currently uses to communicate (i.e., phone, fax, mail, overnight delivery, etc.).

Allowing your customers Internet access to your company can have a number of positive effects:

☆ Efficiency within your business in reviewing and responding to these communications.

☆ Demonstrating your desire to help your customer save money (e.g., your customer does not need to send you information overnight).

☆ Allows your customer a direct line to all of your business (e.g., your company could set up an Internet address that goes directly to the President; president@mycompany.com).

Are your customers geographically dispersed or centrally located?

If all of your customers are local and in close proximity to one another, there may be less of a benefit to using the Internet for day-to-day communications. A fact of life in many businesses is that most people buy from people, and specifically, people they like. If this is true of your business and customers, then a natural follow-up to this axiom is that face-to-face interaction is difficult to improve upon. A lot can depend on what and how you sell. What you sell may not be easy to change, but how you sell is something that always can be improved upon.

If you have customers that are geographically dispersed, then the Internet provides an absolutely wonderful mechanism for two-way communications. If you make sales calls and travel to your customers now, you will still do so. Through the Internet, you could have an additional mechanism to communicate either business-to-business or person-to-person without being intrusive, filling up people's phone mail, or sending faxes.

Are your customers typically businesses or individuals?

One objective of any change or addition you consider making in your business is to increase your customer base. There are two basic types of customers: businesses and individuals. Both represent special considerations when evaluating the possible business benefits of the Internet.

Can you grow your customer base by using the Internet? Perhaps. Regardless of whether you sell to businesses or individuals, keep in mind that businesses are made up of individual people. If you sell to businesses, for example, and a potential customer has an employee who, as an individual, is on the Internet, he or she may find your offering and take it to their place of work. The opposite is also true in that an individual, while at work doing some part of his or her job on the Internet, may find your offering and be prompted to become a customer of yours as an individual. The Internet offers a medium to people, both in a business setting and as individuals.

Businesses

If your company markets and sells to other businesses, then the business benefits of the Internet have slightly more appeal today, although this may be reversed within a year as individual users are flocking to the Internet by the thousands.

Most businesses, and quite possibly most of your customers, have some type of computer system. Even most

Customers

small businesses have personal computers (PCs), and the majority of those have them connected with Local Area Networks (LANs). Also, the odds are that those businesses that do not have any computers are contemplating getting one, and those that have unconnected PCs are contemplating LANs.

Beyond a computer, connection to the Internet basically requires a phone line and some relatively inexpensive software.

The costs are relatively low, and the benefits are relatively easy to obtain. For example, if you send documents to customers via overnight delivery (or they send them to you), an entry level Internet connection for e-mail alone would pay for itself very quickly with the savings of overnight delivery charges.

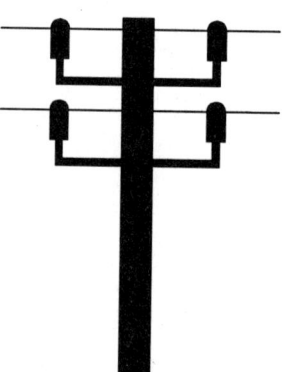

Additionally, business-to-business communication could be enhanced by applying any or all of the above mentioned Internet Applications to your Business Applications.

Business-to-business Internet usage has one immediately clear benefit over businesses that sell to individuals: you can tell your customers it is there and promote its use. You can let your customers know you can be reached electronically, and that it will save them time and money to use that method. This is exactly what is happening over and over today, and is a primary reason why there are so many businesses rushing to the Internet. This is a main reason why business managers today are feeling like they need to be on the Internet immediately.

Individuals

If your company targets individuals in marketing and sales, there is an issue to deal with that can be tricky. How do you let everyone know how to get to you?

Customers

The Internet is huge (250,000+ destinations). How do you make yourself stand out among this crowd?

Depending on your average customer profile, this may be easy or it may be almost impossible. For example, if you know that a certain percentage of your customers are computer literate (e.g., use PCs regularly), then you have a fairly safe bet in marketing to them through the Internet. This is true primarily because of the onslaught of individuals hooking up to the Internet to explore. If any of these people happen to buy your products or are prospects, then simply advertising that you are on the Internet will lead them to you.

This holds true for a very simple reason. With over 250,000 places to go on the Internet, the average Internet user can be as confused as anyone else trying to get around. If this person happens to know and have interest in your product or product type, then he or she is a prime candidate to find you on the Internet if you tell him or her where to look. This requires "advertising your advertisement" in mediums other than the Internet. For example, in your next print ad, if you announced that all of your product information was now available on the Internet (and where to find you), you would find that your prospects/customers would look you up.

If your average customer is not a computer user, you are most likely limited to using the Internet for purposes other than directly connecting to the people who buy from you.

How "computer literate" are your customers?

Right now, the degree of computer literacy in your customer base is an important variable in determining how much time and money you will spend, if any, on the Internet.

Recall that the Internet is comprised of computers and people. There are many computers on the Internet around the

Customers

clock without human intervention. There are no people on the Internet, however, without computers.

Since your prospects/customers are most likely not computers themselves, unless you can get to the people who buy your products through a computer, you will have limited revenue success on the Internet.

Do not conclude that there is not a use of the Internet for your business just because your customers do not use computers. There are many other benefits of using the Internet, and many other ways to succeed on it. However, most of these will take the form of internal productivity increases and industry knowledge.

Chapter Six

Products

As with the assessment of your customers, assessing your products is another area to explore when determining justification for putting your business on the Internet.

Do you sell "soft" products?

The term "soft" products is meant to describe just about anything other than a physical product that consumes space and has weight. Examples include:

Information — Prime examples are consultants who provide informational services (e.g., research followed by a document outlining analysis and/or recommendations).

Computer Services — Programming, data entry, tuning, performance monitoring, etc.

Documents — Books, lists, reference materials, drawings, etc.

Software — Regardless of hardware type, model, etc.

Data — Mailing lists, reference lists, etc., that are sold on diskette or tape.

Products

All of the above can be delivered electronically. Most businesses that work in the "soft" product industries are using computers to design, build, and/or maintain their products. Using the Internet is a natural and cost-effective extension to those businesses.

Do you sell physical goods?

Whether your business sells "soft" products or not, there are some commonalties to all sales, regardless of product type. Everything in the sales process, except the actual delivery of the physical product, can be managed through the Internet. Ordering, credit approval, order acknowledgment, order status, warranty registration, and customer feedback are just a few of the areas which can support the sales of physical goods.

If you do sell physical goods, then pictures of the products may be an important component of your marketing. The Internet provides a simple method of delivering pictures and text directly to the desktop of your customers.

Do you support the end-users of these products?

Post-sale activities are commonly the driving factor for repeat business and word-of-mouth reference sales.

Your business's ability to effectively support your products after the sale can be critical in any competitive market. Post-sales support can include:

♦ Warranty registration (and acknowledgment of registration).

♦ Product notices.

♦ Product update notification and/or distribution.

♦ New product announcements.

- Managing feedback, suggestions, comments, complaints, etc.

- Notification of price changes, policy updates, etc.

- Communication with hotline support personnel.

Depending on what you do now, utilizing the Internet for any or all of the above can improve, or at least supplement, the processes. For example, if you have a warranty registration card that is included with your products, include a space for your "Internet address." You may find that you have a large percentage of customers who use the Internet, and you will immediately have another avenue to contact them.

Another sample application is to publish a "feedback avenue" for your customers which allows them to give input, comments, suggestions, etc., directly to the management of your company (e.g., send e-mail to president@mycompany.com). This clearly demonstrates that you care about your customers' ideas.

How many product categories do you have? How many line items?

When considering business Internet usage, an examination of your product line is a fundamental exercise.

Consider how you categorize your products, and how you might better categorize them. If you currently categorize your products into two categories—goods and services—and you have 2,000 line items, then you would create a gigantic electronic mess on the Internet trying to communicate and describe what you do.

When putting product information on the Internet, the product lines should be cleanly categorized, with a simple,

Products

clear overview of the categories. This enables a customer or prospective customer to quickly see what product areas are available, and determine if or what areas they want to explore.

If your business is like many out there today (and I hope it is not), then this is not a trivial exercise. Unfortunately, many businesses are in a relatively poor shape when it comes to cleanly managed product information. This is typically not anyone's "fault" in particular. It is the unfortunate result of the natural evolution of a business. As employees come and go, products change, brochures change, and so on, clean management of product information can take a back seat to getting business done today.

Before deciding to actually promote products on the Internet, clear categories, descriptions, and overviews are a necessity.

Chapter Seven

Marketing

For the following discussion, a clear distinction is assumed between marketing and sales. Although both are intertwined and mutually dependent functions of an organization, they are separate tasks involving different skills, actions, and processes. This section applies solely to marketing, meaning the process by which you let customers and prospects know about you and your offers.

If there is any one particularly hot business area that holds promise for the Internet, it is in marketing. Just about any and all forms of product marketing are being put onto the Internet at astounding rates. Of the 250,000+ existing destinations on the Internet, and the 6,000+ per month that are being added, the vast majority are being put there for one marketing purpose or another.

A clear set of marketing objectives is helpful when implementing a marketing campaign on the Internet. Do you want to market your company with a company history and overview section? Do you want to market your products? The types of products you offer? The value-added components of your products? Every product line item? Your services? Do you want to provide samples of your products (e.g., "soft" products)?

There are a number of things to consider, and a number of real and mythical benefits. Marketing on the Internet is an area that requires extra effort on the part of the business doing the marketing. Doing the wrong thing (i.e., violating netiquette) can result not only in an ineffective marketing campaign, but near violent response towards your company from would-be customers.

Internet users primarily look to the Internet for information. They want to browse, shop, compare, and perhaps buy, but on their terms and at their pace. They do not take kindly to being surprised with advertisements for products unless they are browsing with a particular kind of product in mind.

For example, posting an advertisement of your company's newest hairspray in one of the football forums because you think that most people who watch football use hairspray will likely result in a fair amount of nasty e-mail, phone calls, and hatred from all of the avid football fans on the Internet (regardless of whether they are hairspray users or not).

Consider the following questions when assessing the possibility of marketing on the Internet:

Do you advertise now?

If you advertise now, where do you do it? Ads, mailings, TV, radio, billboards? If you have some idea about what is the most effective type of advertising for your business, then you have a head start in determining what will be most effective on the Internet.

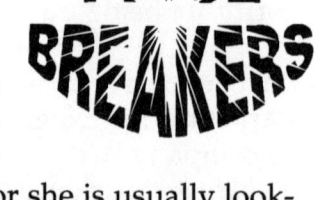

Catchy, trendy, eye-popping print ads may have limited appeal on the Internet. If the average Internet user is browsing around the network, he or she is usually looking for something of interest, and not necessarily in the same mindset as they might be when flipping casually through a magazine or newspaper.

Although the Internet can technically handle audio and

video, there are very few end-users who have the equipment required to effectively "play" this type of information.

When considering any type or format of advertisement in general, you must first put yourself in the shoes of the potential target person of the advertisement. On the Internet, people are usually fairly focused on their computer screen and are relatively active in reading the information that is there.

Catchy graphics definitely help, but like anything else, they can be used to an excess. Graphics are a two-edged sword on the Internet. Keep in mind that the average target person of the ad is more than likely connected to the Internet by a phone line. This means that there is a limit to how fast information gets to their computer screen, and graphics are notorious for taking a long time to retrieve and display. However, if the information a business puts on the Internet has no graphics at all, then it immediately appears to be difficult to digest.

There is a developing school of Internet ergonomics relating to just about every type of information on the Internet. The objective is to make it easy for the user to find you and display a short, descriptive, and interest-provoking overview screen. If interested, the user can go deeper into the information. At that point, your information can get more detailed and graphical, since the user will now be proactively digging for more information. 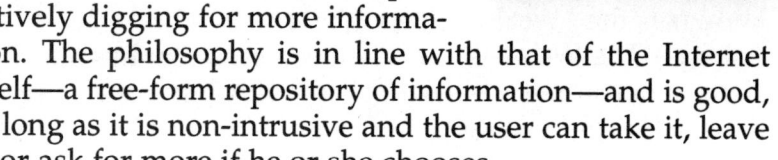 The philosophy is in line with that of the Internet itself—a free-form repository of information—and is good, as long as it is non-intrusive and the user can take it, leave it, or ask for more if he or she chooses.

Unsolicited information is generally considered a bad thing on the Internet. Many people are learning the hard way that blanketing users with e-mail is not always a good idea. It sounds great, since the idea is that you create some information about what you want to sell and then play the numbers. If you send it to 1,000 people, then perhaps 5 will buy. If you send it to 10,000 people, then 50 will buy. That may be true for other forms of marketing, but on the Internet if you send something unsolicited to 10,000 people, you will most likely make 10,000 people angry enough to remember your company and never buy anything from you again.

There are right ways and wrong ways to advertise on the Internet. There are effective and ineffective ways as well. There are discussion groups, for example, that are specifically put there for the purpose of advertising and describing your product. The best way to do it is to create a presence on the Internet with something called a *Home Page* after you have determined that your prospects are candidates for an Internet-based ad.

A Home Page is a *destination* on the Internet that is formatted with a document scripting language. Do not be afraid of this language as if it were a computer programming language. It is really quite simple to learn. The point of a Home Page is to publish its address so that your customers and prospects can browse their way to it whenever they  like. This is non-intrusive and gives your business complete control over its content and appearance.

By posting a Home Page on the Internet, a business immediately becomes part of what is called the "Web," also known as the "World Wide Web," or "WWW." This terminology—The Web—is one of those terms that has all of the signs of becoming a household word. Anything and everything appears to be there. You would be very hard pressed to think up a subject that is not addressed on The Web.

The Web contains literally millions of individual documents, graphics, and electronic forms which reside on thousands of computers that all know how to talk to each other.

Each document has an address and typically contains the addresses of other documents within it. For example, a Home Page document on the subject of zoos may contain some flashy graphics of exotic animals and a listing of popular zoos around the world. If the user, while viewing this document, points his or her cursor (i.e., mouse pointer) to the highlighted phrase "San Diego Zoo," the Internet will automatically go the address of the San Diego Zoo's Home Page and allow the user to view that document.

These links between documents are called Hotlinks, which work similarly to the Help system in Microsoft Windows. If you are familiar with Microsoft Windows, then you know that while viewing help on subject XYZ, you can point and click on a highlighted phrase within the help document and immediately view more detailed information on the item you selected.

A Home Page is not free, and many businesses rushing out to build themselves a Home Page are subjecting themselves to Information SuperHighway robbery. There are many companies out there selling Home Page space and Home Page services. As more and more businesses learn about the Internet, the companies that overcharge for this service will disappear. In the meantime, as a business manager, you at least have to hold some respect for them for being smart enough to capitalize on a booming market.

Do you do mailings?

As discussed earlier, mass mailings are not a good thing on the Internet. As good as it sounds to be able to create one message and send it to thousands, if not millions, of recipients with one stroke of a key, the harm a business can cause itself can be irreparable.

There is a popular story in circulation about a couple who were both attorneys specializing in immigration. They felt the Internet might be a perfect place to advertise their services. The Internet is, after all, a worldwide medium where you can reach millions of potential clients in other countries, without ever buying a plane ticket or an advertisement done in another language. What they did made Internet history.

As the story goes, they posted an advertisement-oriented message in every discussion group they could find, regardless of the discussion group topic. They did indeed reach millions of people worldwide with one stroke of the keyboard. However, of the millions who saw their message, most were infuriated by the intrusion. The two attorneys immediately received so much electronic hate mail that, it is alleged, the computer they were connected to crashed due to the volume. They were deluged from every angle for doing something in complete violation of netiquette.

So what did they do? They quit being immigration attorneys and went into the "how-to-advertise-on-the-Internet" business. They wrote a book on the subject and are one of the many groups now making millions of dollars hyping the Internet.

Mailings to your customer base, however, is something altogether different. Typically an ongoing customer will appreciate getting information through the Internet. Notice of newsletters, announcements, upgrades, seminars, etc., are all typically well received by existing customers. If not, they will usually reply to your message asking to be removed from your mailing list. If this happens, you should most definitely remove them.

Do you produce catalogs or brochures with pictures & graphics?

If your business now produces catalogs, brochures, spec sheets, or any form of printed material describing your

Marketing

offerings, then the Internet could be an ideal vehicle for publishing.

Pictures and graphics are not prohibitive as long as their placement is done with some forethought. In fact, pictures and graphics are necessary, even something as simple as a company logo.

Assuming that your customers and prospects are on the Internet, the business benefits of putting product information on the Internet are clear.

✦ Production costs decrease.

✦ Customers and prospects can print them if they like, or review them on-line.

✦ A built-in feedback mechanism is easy to implement, thereby allowing a customer or prospect to read information and immediately ask questions through electronic mail.

✦ Management of the information is as easy, if not easier, as what you do now.

✦ Dynamic updates are inherent to the medium. As prices, products, policies, etc., change, these changes are reflected in your materials immediately.

Do you use forms for prospects to complete?

Does your company, like most others, handle a lot of forms? Do your customers fill out forms? Do your prospects fill out forms asking for more information?

The Internet provides a facility that not only allows browsing of information and communication through electronic mail, but on-line forms completion as well.

Marketing

Fill-in-the-blank and multiple choice forms are a feature of the Hypertext language used to create Home Pages, providing yet another method of information gathering and communication for your company.

Examples of form usage that can provide business benefits include:

- Forms for prospects to complete indicating who they are, their interests, etc.

- Information request forms.

- Order forms.

- Customer information update forms (i.e., new address, phone, etc.).

- Warranty registration forms.

- Customer questionnaires.

Just about any form you now use in hard copy format can be made available on the Internet, potentially saving time for both your company and your customers and prospects.

Do you produce press releases for the media?

Communicating with the press is always a challenge, and is accomplished in a variety of ways including mailings, fax broadcasts, wining and dining, phone tag, etc.

The press, across all industries, was one of the first to take advantage of the Internet. Writers, editors, and publishers all work with printed text and graphics, and all of them use computers these days for producing their product. They are accustomed to acquiring, distributing, and communicating electronically, and the Internet has provided them a global vehicle for doing so.

Marketing

Many members of the press now publish their Internet IDs so that they can be reached through the Internet. These folks expect to receive information through the Internet, and in fact, most prefer it.

Sending press releases through the Internet to members of the press is not only acceptable, but is very efficient and effective.

Marketing on the Internet is an exploding Business Application. The effectiveness of Internet marketing is highly dependent on a number of variables, but this represents the fastest growing and potentially most effective Business Application on the Internet.

Chapter Eight

Sales

The Internet can be a good medium for assisting your sales department and boosting company sales. After all, an increase in sales is a main reason you're exploring your options for getting on the Internet, isn't it? Ask yourself the following questions to help match up your business with Internet capabilities:

Does your business have a sales force?

If so, then there is typically an ongoing effort to communicate with them, to them, and through them. You want to ensure that they understand your product offerings and communicate them clearly.

Internal business communication with the sales force is a natural business application of the Internet.

It is always helpful for both management and the sales force to get everyone together regularly. This is not always easy, since many sales forces are geographically dispersed, may be comprised of agents, or hopefully, they are busy making sales calls. Regardless of the effort required, it is usually beneficial to get together for the following reasons:

Sales

➲ Communicate new products, sales strategies, offerings, etc.

➲ Document pricing policies, rate changes, etc.

➲ Provide ego-reward (which all sales people enjoy) to leading sales people.

➲ Share success stories, references, etc.

➲ Discuss and brainstorm on how to overcome real-world objections.

All of the above can be accomplished on a regular basis via the Internet. The combination of e-mail and Home Pages which outline product information make regular communication easy. This certainly does not take the place of face-to-face meetings, but increasing the regularity of information flow is definitely beneficial to sales forces.

Lead distribution is a specific communication that goes on regularly in companies that have sales forces. After a marketing department has generated leads as a result of a campaign, the timely distribution, tracking, and follow-up on those leads is critical.

Also, sales people typically provide regular feedback to management in the form of call reports, forecasts, customer feedback, etc. A sales person with a PC can use a spreadsheet and/or word processor to create the information, and then send it via e-mail. This Business Application has numerous benefits, including:

▼ Sales people can send or receive information any time of day, so their selling time does not have to be impacted to communicate with management.

▼ Reports, forecasts, and any information created on a PC can be sent as is, so that the receiver can modify, merge, and manipulate it if he or she likes (e.g., instead of sending forecasts via fax, the spreadsheet forecast can be sent in electronic spreadsheet format so that the sales manager can easily combine it with the others to create an overall forecast).

Does your business have sales support people?

Sales support organizations, regardless of being internal or in the field, need to communicate much like others in the company. They typically need to communicate not only with the sales people, but with each other as well.

Increasing the communication in a sales support organization can have immediate benefits. For example, if a sales support person in California spent 20 hours last month finding a solution to a particular problem for a customer, the communication of the problem and solution could save other support people 20 hours this month or the next.

The ability to create a central repository of sales support information is a definite business benefit of the Internet.

Many companies now do this internally in a variety of ways. The Internet provides a simple, consistent method for communicating, storing, and managing this type of information.

The business of sales force automation is predicted to be a multi-billion dollar industry by the year 2000. There are enormous benefits to be gained through sales force automation. Combining other areas of business automation directly with sales force automation can provide significant benefits to a business.

Chapter Nine

Suppliers

Just as your customers might benefit from communicating with your business through the Internet, you, as a customer, can realize those same benefits in dealings with your suppliers.

As more and more businesses move onto the Internet, you will undoubtedly find that your suppliers will be there. They are interested in the same benefits that you are interested in, and you can both realize them together.

The relationship between a typical supplier and his or her customer is usually one where both know exactly what they want, the pricing, policies, and ordering procedures. Conducting this type of business transaction via the Internet could quickly increase efficiency, provide immediate feedback (e.g., inventory status), and eliminate a great deal of paperwork that both parties now go through in the normal course of business.

Chapter Ten

International

If you do business internationally, want to do business internationally, or even have a need to communicate internationally, then the Internet offers an easy method of getting there.

The costs of phone, mail, and especially overnight delivery to international locations is extremely high. The Internet is truly a worldwide communications vehicle. There are no additional costs or requirements to communicate internationally. Sending an e-mail to a destination in France is the same as sending one across town.

Geographical location has nothing to do with any Internet user accessing information your business posts on the Internet. If you were to provide a Home Page on the Internet, it would be just as easy for a prospect in Israel to get your information as it would be for a prospect in your same city.

There are, however, some issues relating to international use of

International

the Internet that businesses should be aware of. The Internet is not a way around import/export laws, tariffs, and duties. If you plan on actually delivering products ("soft" or physical products) internationally, there are certain procedures that apply, directly relating to the applicable international trade laws and regulations. This guide does not explore the specific laws and regulations you must follow in order to do business internationally. There are many sources of information on those topics. However, this guide would be remiss in not making the point that the Internet does not provide a vehicle to circumvent international trade regulations.

Excluding the issue of actual product delivery, the Internet provides a relatively inexpensive way to test market your products in other countries. If you begin to receive e-mail from international Internet users asking about your products, then you may want to further invest in international trade.

You may or may not have potential international customers contact you, but you may very well have potential international distributors, resellers, or business partners contact you. There are many businesses in other countries that import and resell U.S. products. These businesses are learning about the Internet just like you, and may very well use it as a form of product sourcing.

Chapter Eleven

Technical

When all is said and done regarding business on the Internet, a review of the technology requirements is inevitable. You may now have a number of ideas on business Internet usage as it applies to your company. There are two basic types of investments that must be made in order to do business on the Internet. One is in skills, the other may be in technology.

Asking some basic questions will help you understand what you need to know before you can go forward. Also, understanding your technical options and the associated benefits and limitations of each is a foundation of business Internet usage.

Options

There are many options for getting on the Internet. Each option has pros and cons, and associated costs. In addition to the trouble of keeping up with the sheer number of available options, these options are changing rapidly as time goes on. There is good news in this message, however:

> 💻 Because there are many options, there is much flexibility. You could start small and grow into the Internet as a function of the success you find along the way.

Technical

🖥 You can outsource the entire process, thereby limiting your investment until you learn more.

🖥 You can use just about any kind of computer. Unlike many things in the technology world, the Internet does not require a special type of computer (e.g., DOS, Windows, Macintosh, etc.).

Listing every available option would make this document extremely lengthy and effectively out-of-date within a week. A specific technical recommendation on what your business should do would require a more detailed analysis of what you have now and what you want to accomplish.

Both the most popular options available and the components that are required can be broken down into categories. A listing of the possible components are as follows:

Component	**Description**	**Source(s)**
Personal Computer	• IBM PC or compatible	• Computer stores
	• Apple Macintosh	
Modem	• A computer attachment that allows the computer to communicate over phone lines	• Computer stores
Phone line	• Standard phone lines for voice communications work for Internet data communications as well	
Internet Access Software	• Software that connects your computer to an	• Computer stores

Technical

	Internet Access Provider and supports the Internet Applications (e-mail, browser, file transfer, etc.)	• Prices are in the $30 to $150 range • (see Appendix B for more information on these packages)
Internet Access Providers	• The service that your computer calls into • These services provide a passageway into the Internet around the clock	• There are many service providers available today • Prices typically include a monthly fee ($5 to $50) and/or an hourly connection fee ($5 to $15) • (see Appendix D for more information on these service companies)
Internet Server Services 	• These are companies that you can rent space and time from on their equipment, thereby giving the impression to the Internet community that you have your own Internet hardware connection	• Many Internet Access Providers also offer this service • Prices typically include an upfront fee ($100-$2,000), a monthly fee ($25-$500), and/or a space usage fee (depending on how much information you put on their machine)

Technical

Internet Server Hardware	• Your own physical machine and connection into the Internet	• This may be a computer you already have, with the addition of a dedicated phone line
		• New systems, ready to go right out of the box are in the $6,000-$15,000 range
		• A dedicated phone line connection ranges from $500-$2,000 per month, depending on the speed and capacity of the line
Internet Server Software	• The software that is run on an Internet Server Hardware platform	• If you were to purchase and implement Internet Server Hardware, the software is typically included in the price of the hardware package

As you can clearly see, the cost range is quite varied. A simple connection can cost as little as $20 plus a nominal monthly access and/or usage fee. A high-end connection, with your own server, can cost $15,000-$20,000 or more just for the equipment to begin, plus the ongoing high-speed communication lines.

The old adage regarding fools—"there's one born every minute"—applies to business on the Internet just like anything else. As hard as it is to believe, there are dozens of small companies which have almost no business justification for being on the Internet that have purchased computer hardware, installed and reworked networks, and signed up for ongoing five-figure monthly communication bills in order to be on the Internet. Hopefully, you are not one of them.

As with most things, a clear vision of your objectives will help you determine what is right for your business. And like many other things as well, what is right for you is usually somewhere in the middle of the two ends of the spectrum.

The following table generally categorizes the various options into three broad levels: Internet access levels, their capabilities, and the components required.

Internet Access Level	Capabilites	Components Required
Entry Level	• E-mail • Ability to browse and explore the Internet	• Personal Computer • Modem • Phone Line • Internet Access Software
Mid Level	• E-mail • Ability to browse and explore the Internet	• Personal Computer • Modem • Phone Line • Internet Access Software
High Level	• E-mail • Ability to browse and explore the Internet	• Internet Access Provider • Internet Server Hardware

Technical

| High Level (cont.) | • Unlimited business presence on the Internet (outside access directly into your system, for example, to place orders or check inventory) | • Dedicated phone line |

Before deciding on any of the options or combinations thereof, an inventory of your business computing equipment is highly recommended.

Some of the questions to ask are:

⊛ Do you have personal computers now? How old/new are they (80386, 486, etc.)?

⊛ Are they connected with a Local Area Network? What kind? What server(s)?

⊛ Do you use e-mail now? What type?

⊛ Do you have designated staff to maintain computer(s)?

⊛ Do all of the areas of your business use the same software packages (i.e., Lotus, Microsoft, etc.)?

⊛ What is the general computer literacy of departments?

⊛ Do you use modems to connect to outside services now?

Depending on how you answer these questions, you may be ready to get into the Internet at a high level at a very low cost, or you may have a relatively high cost to get into the Internet at a low level.

Regardless of how you assess your company's technology, there are two points to keep in mind regarding the technical costs

Technical

involved in business Internet usage:

1. As more and more people use the Internet, the connection costs will decrease.

2. As more and more people use technology in general, computer hardware and software costs will decrease.

So, if you are not able to financially manage getting onto the Internet today, you may be able to in a matter of months.

Chapter Twelve

Your Competitors

What are your competitors doing on the Internet? Has it helped their businesses? How, exactly, are they using the Internet?

There is one sure way to find out what your competitors are doing—get on the Internet at an entry level and browse around to see.

Another way is to wait and see if your customers start asking you about your plans on the Internet. If you get this question, you may very well have a competitor targeting your customer base. If you are the ABC Company, for example, consider what your competitor might tell your customer if he or she were offering business applications on the Internet. He or she might say, "Mr. Customer...":

▶ Do you ever play phone-tag with ABC Company just to get a simple question answered?

▶ Do you always have the latest product information and/or pricing from ABC Company?

▶ Do you feel that you can communicate your impression of ABC Company and their products to ABC Company management?

Your Competitors

➤ Do you spend money, time, and resources on sending information to or getting information from ABC Company?

➤ Have you ever paid for an overnight package of information to be sent to ABC Company?

➤ How do you access ABC Company's support organization?

➤ How do you place orders with ABC Company?

➤ How do you check the status of orders with ABC Company?

➤ Have you ever not been able to take advantage of a special offering or promotion from ABC Company because they didn't communicate it to you (for whatever reason)?

If the thought of a competitor asking these questions to your customers is at all unsettling, then you might want to get in front now. Your competitors are not going to let you know what they are doing, and if service is important in your business, then the Internet is a vehicle that can help improve it (even implemented at an entry level).

Perception is reality, and the perception that you can create by allowing customers to communicate with you electronically is a good one. It shows that your organization is efficient and intelligent, and that you know how to take advantage of technology to save yourself, and your customers, time and money.

Chapter Thirteen

Security

With all of the alleged business occurring on the Internet, a very good question to ask is, "what about security?" Security violations typically get their fair share of media coverage. Newspapers, magazines, and television all seem to report on these violations. There are three basic issues and several potential solutions regarding security. The main issues you must consider are:

1. Securing information (e.g., how do I keep Internet hackers out of my computer system?).

2. Securing transactions (e.g., sending credit card information over the Internet).

3. Securing your people (e.g., how do I keep my employees from playing on the Internet?).

There are a number of solutions to these three issues, as outlined below. There is one important point to note, however, regarding these issues. Internet usage is growing fast, and those using it are demanding solutions to these issues. Necessity breeds invention. Where there are hundreds of thousands of people with the same problem, there are dozens of clever companies out there working on solving it.

Security

Another fact of life in the computing world is this: the only 100%, absolutely, positively, foolproof way to secure something on a computer is to seal the computer in a box full of concrete and throw it in the ocean, then put around-the-clock armed guards on duty above and below the water to guard it. This is true because, theoretically, any security mechanism designed by a human being can be broken, given enough time and energy.

Pragmatically speaking, the average business should not be overly paranoid about security on the Internet. Unless you are in a business involving highly classified and interesting material, the average computer hacker out there could care less about what you are doing. If you do need to be concerned about security, then there are some relatively foolproof ways of attacking the issues.

Securing Information

Securing information is only a concern if you have your own Internet Server Hardware connected into the Internet. If so, you have implemented this system so that people can get to it. That being the case, how do you limit their access?

There are a variety of software and hardware solutions to the problem. All of these solutions fall into a category termed "firewalls." Firewalls are mechanisms designed to keep people out of areas of your computer system(s) that you designate as being protected.

Firewalls are generally quite effective and can provide you with a high level of confidence in their function. They are not cheap. Depending on a variety of factors (software, hardware, degree of protection, etc.), prices can range from one thousand to tens of thousands of dollars.

Securing Transactions

With the rapid increase in actual product purchases over the Internet, people's credit card numbers are being zipped across the nation and across oceans in order to pay for products. Are there

Security

hackers out there waiting to steal these numbers? Most likely there are, but pragmatically speaking, there are relatively few. There are very few reported incidents of this type of theft on the Internet, but as the volume of purchases conducted this way increases, there will certainly be more hackers trying to get in on it.

So, how do you combat the stealing of your customers' credit card numbers? There are generally three options. One is slightly risky, one is foolproof, and the other is just beginning to emerge.

> 1. The slightly risky option is to go ahead and take the credit card number over the Internet. The odds are high that no one will steal the number, but the possibility exists.
>
> 2. The foolproof option is to take the full order over the Internet, and give the customer the option of calling you by phone to give the credit card number. This puts the burden of the security worry on the customer if he or she decides to enter the number on-line, and gives him or her the option of calling you directly to avoid the risk.
>
> 3. The last option is to use one of the many services now becoming available on the Internet. There are companies that specialize in processing transactions, for a fee, over the Internet. They can handle everything for you, including providing the standard Internet Applications (i.e., e-mail, Home Pages, etc.). As this service grows, you can expect dozens, if not hundreds of these services to be available. This includes the big guns; that is, the largest banking and finance institutions in the country are now working furiously to get these services in place.

Securing Your People

If you make a bold move and implement Internet access and availability to all of your employees overnight, what you may get in return is a dramatic hit in productivity around the office. There is so much to do, so many interesting things, and so many special interests available on the Internet, that your employees will inevitably find "their thing" out there somewhere.

Security

Your employees are people, and each person has some special interest. It may be an interest in woodworking, aviation, auto mechanics, or anything else for that matter.

The question is, how do you keep your employees from wasting company time on the Internet? The answer is a difficult one.

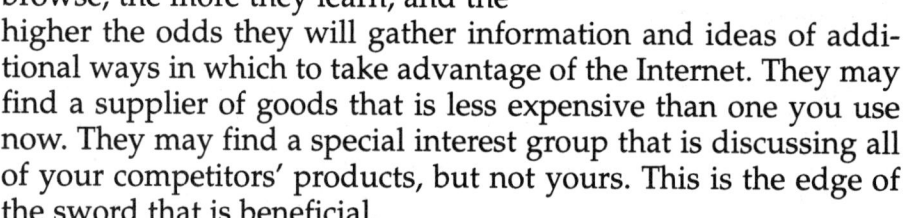

Keep in mind that the fact that your employees would be pro-actively browsing around the Internet is a two-edged sword. The more they browse, the more they learn, and the higher the odds they will gather information and ideas of additional ways in which to take advantage of the Internet. They may find a supplier of goods that is less expensive than one you use now. They may find a special interest group that is discussing all of your competitors' products, but not yours. This is the edge of the sword that is beneficial.

The other edge of the sword is the potential for productivity losses. Once people get comfortable browsing the Internet (which is not a very long time), they can spend hours upon hours poking around.

There are some technical ways in which to attack this issue, but they can be difficult to maintain and can possibly impact any other benefits you are striving for in Internet usage.

The real answer to this issue is management. This is basically a behavior issue. Management does not allow four hour poker games during the day, so why would management tolerate four hours of Internet browsing in non-business-oriented areas. Employees must be made aware that the Internet is put in place for business use, and like other business tools (e.g., copier, supplies, etc.), the Internet is not free. Employees should be cost conscious in other areas of the business, so they should be with Internet usage as well.

After implementation of Internet access for a period of time, management should ask employees what they do on the Internet, what they have found, how has it helped, etc. Also, management review of the connection time and costs on a regular basis can help pinpoint any employee(s) who may have excessive Internet use and limited stated benefits (and perhaps a productivity loss as well).

Security Summary

Overall security on the Internet is a real issue and should be looked at carefully in light of the specific objectives your business has for its use. However, security should not be a deterrent to moving forward if you can identify potential business benefits of Internet utilization.

Secure financial transactions will be available on the Internet in the very near future. Even now there are a number of secure, cost-effective methods of solving these problems. Each of the proposed solutions attack the problem from various angles, including hardware locks, software encoding/decoding, and even digital signatures. Many are even available today. Like many other issues in the technology field, there are many workable ways to skin the cat. The method that is best received by the end-user community is typically the one that wins out as the standard. With the masses apparently racing to the Internet, it won't be long before a standard, workable, cost-effective solution is deemed the standard (i.e., when everyone uses it, it is standard, regardless of what IBM, the government, or anyone else thinks about it).

Chapter Fourteen

Making the Decisions

Should your business be on the Internet? I would suggest that there are three possible answers:

No

"No" is fine. If you feel some pressure to "be on it," then simply ignore the pressure and go about your business. You have explored the options, and if you don't see cost justifiable benefits, then your answer to the Internet question is "no."

You may, however, be at least a little curious at this point. If so, and if you have a personal computer, then a small investment in software and connection time can help you dig deeper.

Keep in mind that the Internet is evolving quite rapidly, and your business may be also. The fact that your answer might be "no" right now does not necessarily mean that it will be "no" a year from now.

Yes

If so, then to what degree? At what level should you enter into it?

Making the Decisions

What Business Applications are you interested in?

What areas of your business would you like to see using the Internet?

What are your priorities? Marketing, sales, research, etc.?

How is your business prepared, technically, to be on the Internet?

What additional equipment do you need?

I Don't Know

If you still don't know, then you need to ask yourself "why?"

There are a number of consulting groups that can provide you with more detailed information and service regarding putting your business on the Internet. (Business Architects, Inc. also offers this service. See Appendix F).

If/When You Say YES

By all means, caveat emptor (let the buyer beware)! Shop. Have a list of questions for anyone who is trying to sell you their services, hardware, software, Internet access, or whatever.

The Appendixes of this book appear to have a technical slant, but they are not necessarily "techie." If you think you might want to be on the Internet, then these Appendixes should be required reading. Specific examples and options are outlined regarding what is technically required to be on the Internet.

Additionally, Appendix E is a question & answer worksheet that you should consult when speaking with any vendor offering Internet access, hardware, software, or services.

Lastly, Appendix G outlines what we elected to do in the company I was initially doing research for: what we did, why we did it, where we went wrong, what we did right, what it cost, and some of the results.

Appendix Contents

Appendix A: **Hardware Alternatives** *81*

Appendix B: **Software Alternatives** *85*

Appendix C: **Communications Alternatives** . *91*

Appendix D: **Service Provider Alternatives** . *95*

Appendix E: **Questions for Internet Service Providers** *99*

Appendix F: **More Detailed Analysis** *105*

Appendix G: **An Example** *107*

Glossary *111*

Appendix A

Hardware Alternatives

Depending on exactly what you want to accomplish, your computer hardware requirements may be quite simple or quite complex. This Appendix outlines the various options, the general costs, and what they provide. Additionally, some specific examples are given.

There are literally dozens of hardware options for connection to the Internet, and they are constantly changing. For general discussion, however, there are two basic options:

1. Individual Access.

2. Your Own Internet Server.

Both of these options are discussed below.

This information is essentially an outline of options available and known at the time of preparation of this book. It would be nearly impossible to detail all of the hardware options available and keep it current.

Computer hardware, in general, is a fast moving technology and business. As such, there is a possibility that the options described

Hardware Alternatives

herein will be unavailable or even out-of-date by the time you are reviewing this information. This being the case, this information is being outlined as general and specific as possible with the goal of not being too general (i.e., pragmatically worthless), or too specific (i.e., highly probable of being out-of-date in a matter of 3-6 months).

Individual Access

Individual access (for either personal or business use) is primarily provided through dial-up services using standard phone lines and personal computers.

Theoretically, given an Internet access provider, anyone with a personal computer of just about any type, no matter how old, could be on the Internet. That being said, the older PC's (e.g., 8088, 8086, 80286), are akin to driving a horse and buggy down the autobahn—you will move forward and eventually get where you want to go, but it will take a long time, be relatively painful and unfulfilling, and you won't be able to take advantage of the high-speed driving lanes they make available.

Practically speaking, for dial-in access to the Internet and the ability to access the Web, a PC should minimally have:

⇒ 8 Mb memory (minimum—the more the better). If you are buying a PC, keep in mind that for general user happiness, the more memory you get the better.

⇒ 9600 bps modem (minimum—14.4 or 28.8 are better). If you are buying a modem and plan on using the Internet (personal or business), then I suggest a 28.8 modem. You will be very happy you did when you begin moving from document to document within the Web.

⇒ A graphical display and interface. The dominating display types are VGA and SVGA. The dominating interface types are Microsoft Windows (for IBM PC compatibles), Apple Macintosh, X-Windows (for Unix systems), and, to a lesser extent, OS/2 from IBM.

➲ A mouse pointing device is effectively mandatory for using a graphical interface and navigating the Internet.

Your Own Internet Server

Installing a computer for dedicated Internet access should be cost justified and not mistaken as a simple process (regardless of what the advertisements and/or salesman says). That being said, I will certainly eat my words in time.

There are a number of vendors providing software and hardware combinations built explicitly for businesses wanting to plug them into the Internet. There are two issues with these systems (and having your own server in general) that a business should consider:

1. Unix Is Not Easy - The Internet is primarily Unix-based systems talking to Unix-based systems. Unix is not, has not, and most likely will never be known for its user friendliness. But if you want a truly reliable Internet server, then Unix is clearly the choice. Other non-Unix systems are quickly gaining ground (e.g., Microsoft Windows), but for general stability in operation, Unix is the winner.

2. Constant Change - The Internet is changing so rapidly that in order to maintain and keep up with it, your own Internet server will most likely require your own Internet server programmer.

At the time of the writing of this book, the leading supplier of "turn-key" Internet servers was Sun. Sun is selling a combination hardware/software package that has everything required for a server to be connected to the Internet.

The feedback on hardware/software package offerings is generally quite good, but don't be surprised when the extras pop up. Although package offerings in this market claim to have "everything" required, there are requirements outside of the server that are mandatory.

Hardware Alternatives

These extras can include the following:

Router — The device that dynamically keeps tables of other computers' addresses on the Internet, and manages the actual routing of information and/or requests for information from one system to another.

CSU/DSU or Modem — The device that connects the router and/or computer to the communication carrier's lines.

Networking Hardware — Depending on how "connected" you get (e.g., one computer or all computers), you may need to implement or upgrade a Local Area Network (LAN) in your organization.

Summary

For Internet connection hardware, the first place to look is at what you have now. If you are unsure, it is far less expensive to hire a consultant to help you for a day or so in reviewing what you have and what you want to accomplish.

Appendix B

Software Alternatives

When selecting software, determining what you want to accomplish first is equally important, if not more so, than when selecting hardware.

As with hardware alternatives, there are literally dozens of software options for connection to the Internet, and they too are constantly changing. This state of constant change is common in the technology industry in general, but is more pronounced in the software arena than in the hardware arena. For general discussion, however, there are two basic options:

1. Internet User Software.

2. Internet Server Software.

Both of these options are discussed below.

This information is essentially an outline of options available and known at the time of preparation of this book. It is beyond the scope of this book to detail all of the software options currently available.

Computer hardware, in general, is a fast moving technology and

Software Alternatives

business. As such, there is a possibility that the options described herein will be unavailable or even out-of-date by the time you are reviewing this information. This being the case, this information is being outlined as general and specific as possible with the goal of not being too general (i.e., pragmatically worthless), or too specific (i.e., highly probable of being out-of-date in a matter of 3-6 months).

Internet User Software

As an Internet user, you have three basic requirements:

1. Personal Computer (with sufficient capacity, modem, mouse, etc.).

2. Internet Access Provider (the company that your computer dials into in order to get on the Internet).

3. Internet User Software (most often termed "Client" software).

The popular Internet Applications and the software modules required for each are listed below:

Internet Application	Client Module	Description
E-Mail	Internet E-Mail Package	Software that manages your electronic mailbox, allowing you to view, compose, send, reply, forward, save, and print e-mail messages.
Internet Browsing	Web Browser	Software that enables you to view the Home Page documents available on the

Software Alternatives

		World Wide Web (WWW).
Discussion/News Groups	News Group Software	Software that provides connection to popular News Group services and allows you to read as well as post messages to these systems.
File Retrieval	File Transfer Protocol (FTP) Software	Software that provides connection to a wide variety of systems that warehouse files (e.g., programs, documents, etc.). This software allows the user to view and retrieve information stored in these systems.

The good news is that most of the commercially available software has all of the above included in one package. There are so many that any attempt to list them here would be futile. However, you should note that even though most, if not all, of the packages will include all of the above modules, they are not all the same.

Some packages are easier than others. Some follow one "standard," others follow another. There are many methods available to reaching the same end point—end-user access to the Internet.

I hesitate to recommend one package over another, as everyone's needs and skill levels vary, and they all basically do the job. So, how do you know which one to buy? I suggest the following two general guidelines:

 **Research** - See what the computer magazines recommend. If you are a Microsoft Windows user, find a magazine that targets

Software Alternatives

that audience and look for Internet access software reviews. The same goes for Macintosh, Unix, and OS/2.

◨ **Buy From A Reputable Store** - When you buy a package, make sure that you can return the software within a specified period of time (if not for refund, then for exchange for another package). Don't try to save a couple of dollars by purchasing from a retailer that won't allow software returns. This is never a good idea, since you never really know what the software is going to do for you until you install and use it (all software packages have pretty good marketing on the box that may or may not reflect what the software does in reality).

While on the subject of returning software, there is another important point to remember if you do choose a package, try to install it, and then elect to return it. Depending on how far you got into the installation, you may have been connected to a service provider that could possibly begin billing you for access. Many of the end-user packages available today will automatically connect you to a predetermined service provider (this is a major "gotcha," discussed further in Appendix D).

The automatic connection is a two-edged sword. On one hand, the fact that you can buy a software package, install it, and literally be on the Internet in minutes is wonderful. On the other hand, the default service provider may be overcharging you and you would not know it. This is why shopping for a service provider is perhaps the most important checklist item in getting yourself on the Internet.

Internet Server Software

If you come to the conclusion that your business should have your own server, you should most likely seek out a consultant to help you with the implementation.

You should clearly outline your objectives to the consultant and ensure that your current computer system(s) is reviewed carefully to protect yourself from buying things you don't need. Keep in mind that there are "consultants" who do more than consult. Many consultants also resell certain vendors' hardware and/or software. It is not uncommon for a "consultant" in the computer industry to really be a "salesperson." You may already have what you need, but don't know it. Question the consultant. Make sure that you understand what is going to be accomplished, by when, what information you need to provide, and what the ongoing requirements will be to maintain what the consultant puts in place.

The ongoing maintenance of an Internet server is not a trivial task. You may be led to believe that, once installed and configured, the system simply does its thing all day and night, and you don't have to worry about it. This is, at best, a partial truth.

The Internet is extremely complex, and computer programmers and engineers who can manage it with ease are not easy to find (nor are they cheap). Consider the skills that would potentially be required:

- Knowledge of the hardware system.

- Knowledge of the operating system (most likely Unix, or perhaps Microsoft Windows).

- Local Area Networking skills (both hardware and software).

- Internet server software knowledge:

    - Web/Home Pages.
    - E-Mail.
    - File Transfer Protocol.
    - News Servers.

- Communications.

- Routers.

- End-User Internet software.

Software Alternatives

Keep in mind that there is another option to having your own server that essentially gives your business the same advantages. This option is renting space from a reputable service provider. From all outside appearances, your company can look as if it has its own system directly connected to the Internet, and you let someone else worry about maintaining the technical support and connectivity issues.

Summary

End-user software is relatively inexpensive, widely available, and fairly easy to install and use. Beware of the service provider "gotcha," do a little research, and buy with a return option.

Internet server software can be a giant can of worms and is best dealt with in the company of a trusted and experienced consultant. Unless you have the right skills on staff, the more practical option is to rent space from a service provider.

Appendix C

Communications Alternatives

The options available for communications are a little more clear and defined than for those in the hardware and software arenas. Again, the options can be categorized into two groups: end-user access and Internet server access.

End-User Access

For end-user, individual access, you are pretty much limited to using the phone lines. There are only two questions to be answered: how fast can you transmit/receive information, and what type of phone connection will you use?

The practical bottom limit to a standard modem connection is a speed of 9600. The upper speed limit is 28,800. Additionally, there are a variety of techniques that can make any given speed operate effectively faster than its designation (e.g., data compression methods).

You should not even consider getting on the Internet with less than a 9600 modem connection. If possible, a 14,400 or 28,800 should be used unless you have lots of free time to watch your computer retrieve files (it is not uncommon to spend at least half of your Internet access time waiting for information to be trans-

Communications Alternatives

ferred to your computer).

It is important to note that, as with other issues regarding Internet access, the communications issue is in part related to your Internet access provider. You may, for example, get yourself a 28,800 modem, but your service provider may only be able to handle speeds up to 14,400. If you are paying an hourly access fee, the speed of your connection equates to money out of your pocket.

The question as to the type of connection is not as prevalent today as it will be in the next one to three years. There is a communications technology that has been available for many years, but is not fully implemented or offered by the phone companies. This technology is called ISDN, which allows very high speed digital communications over phone lines. ISDN allows, for example, both voice and data to be carried over the same phone line simultaneously. The problem with ISDN is that, for now, it is not available everywhere and is therefore still relatively expensive when compared to a standard modem and phone line connection.

I mention ISDN here for one reason—it is coming. The phone companies are working to make ISDN as available and affordable as standard phone lines. When this is completed, the ISDN capable modems and software will be in greater demand and prices will drop. You will see ISDN in the coming years and most likely be a user.

Internet Server

Internet servers can be connected to the Internet via a dial-up modem connection just like most end-users do. However, this is generally not a good idea. The volume of traffic that a server can receive can quickly swamp even a 28,800 line.

The volume of traffic that an Internet server receives typically demands higher speed lines that must be leased from the phone company. The various options are:

Communications Alternatives

- ☎ 56 Kbs (pronounced "fifty-six K B S")

- ☎ Fractional T1

- ☎ T1 (pronounced "T One")

- ☎ T3 (pronounced "T Three")

These leased lines are essentially phone lines of increasing capacity, and are protected from the general "noise" that a standard voice phone line can be subjected to.

Leased lines are not dial-up, but rather are dedicated lines that go from one point to another. And unlike a standard dial-up phone line, you don't hang up a leased line. They are always connected, 24 hours a day, seven days a week.

So which one do you select for your server? Again, when dealing with server installations, hiring a consultant is money well spent. Just as there are vendors out there exploiting ignorance in hardware, software, and service offerings, there are those that are actively selling high speed, high bandwidth communications lines to businesses that end up utilizing less than 10% of what they are paying for.

Appendix D

Service Provider Alternatives

The most critical decision that has to be made by anyone wanting to connect to the Internet is which service provider to go with. It is critical because unless you are doing it all yourself, in-house, you will be contracting with someone to provide you a variety of important components:

- E-mail—an address, mailbox, etc.
- Access to the World Wide Web.
- Access to the News Servers.
- Access to file warehousing systems (e.g., FTP sites).
- Home Page space.

Essentially, your service provider is your computer connection into the vast terrain of the Internet. If the provider's system goes down, gets overloaded, or hiccups, you feel it. If, for example, you are relying on the service provider's system to hold e-mail from your customers, what happens if the system crashes and your mail is lost? It holds the potential for business disaster.

Service Provider Alternatives

Given the large degree to which an individual user or business relies on the access provider, there is an important point to be aware of regarding those in the business of being access providers. As the world rushes onto the Internet, access providers are popping up by the truckload. Far too many of them are very small-time operations that are run out of peoples' homes.

A classic example is the service provider who is, in fact, one or two college students or recent graduates. They may be very long on Internet technical expertise, but short on capital for solid hardware and communications lines. This may result in their server being swamped, their phone lines being overloaded, their router crashing, or you receiving busy signals when you attempt to dial in.

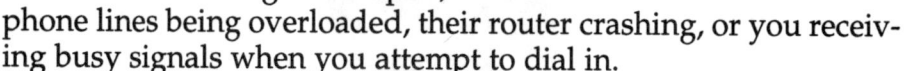

The larger, more reputable service providers have invested in the hardware, communications, and skill levels required to provide solid service. However, beware because many of these organizations are the ones that are overcharging, and they seem intent on doing so until they can no longer get away with it.

The most important thing to do is to shop, and shop wisely. Review Appendix E, which outlines the questions to ask a service provider when shopping.

If you determine that you want business presence on the Internet, then a smart decision to make is to obtain your own domain name. A domain name is the part of the Internet address after the "@". For example:

fbuehler@asystem.net	This Internet address is for F. Buehler at the domain of "asystem.net". The "asystem" is the domain name part. The "net" says that "asystem" is a network access provider.
fbuehler@abc.com	This Internet address is for F. Buehler at the domain of "abc" (for ABC Company, for example). The "com" says that "abc" is a commercial domain on the Internet.

Service Provider Alternatives

There are two main reasons to get your own domain name:

❶ If you determine that you want to get your own server a year from now, or if you want to change Internet Service Providers, the domain name can go with you. If you don't have your own domain name, then you will have to inform everyone you communicate with on the Internet that your address has changed.

❷ If you have your own company domain name, it gives the distinct impression that you have your own system and are taking advantage of technology in your business.

Some service providers offer domain name registration, some do not. Some that offer it are quite reasonably priced, some are absolutely outrageous. Be sure to shop around.

Appendix E

Questions for Internet Service Providers

When shopping the rapidly-growing number of Internet Service Providers, there are several standard questions to ask that will help you:

1. Identify the ones with the specific services and/or features that you need.

2. Separate those that are overcharging from those that are charging a reasonable price.

3. Determine which ones are likely to become technically overloaded with increased use and, in turn, provide you with poor performance.

4. Figure out which ones match up with your business needs and which ones do not.

When you begin your shopping expedition, you should photocopy the following pages and answer each question for each service provider you look into.

A very reasonable question at this point is, "where do I find a list

Questions for Internet Service Providers

of Internet service providers to start shopping?" There are a number of reasons why this question is not easy to accurately answer.

⌨ The number of providers is growing extremely fast. Every day, somewhere in the U.S. and elsewhere in the world, numerous technically-oriented groups of individuals are forming companies that provide Internet access. Some are small, some medium, and some large.

⌨ Not all of these service providers have the same amount of resources, and the resources that they do have may be allocated differently within their company. For example, company "A" may have $50,000 to start their company, so they spend $20,000 on their computer system and $30,000 on marketing. Company "B" may also have $50,000 to start their company, but they spend $45,000 on their computer system and only $5,000 on marketing. If you do not know the proper questions to ask, you may be easily swayed towards the company with the lesser system resources (which is what you are buying in the end), but the better marketing.

⌨ These companies do not all market themselves in the same way. They will advertise themselves in newspapers, computer magazines, through seminars, mailings, and any other way they can think of.

A thorough shopping spree will be comprised of three components:

1. Keep an eye open in your local newspaper for Internet Service Provider advertisements.

Questions for Internet Service Providers

2. Go to the bookstore or library and get a copy of the most recent book that specifically lists every known provider at the time of the book's printing (these books are never completely up-to-date, but they are a very good source of information).

3. When it fits in your daily conversations, ask anyone and everyone if they are on the Internet. If they are, find out who their service provider is and if they are happy with them. Get the provider's name and number and go through the checklist.

Name _____ Phone _____

City, State _____

ACCESS FEES

Sign Up Fee:	❑ NO	❑ YES	$ _____
Set Up Fee:	❑ NO	❑ YES	$ _____
Monthly Fee:	❑ NO	❑ YES	$ _____
Hourly Fee:	❑ NO	❑ YES	$ _____
Fee per # of Accesses:	❑ NO	❑ YES	$ _____
Other Fees:	❑ NO	❑ YES	$ _____

DOMAIN NAME FEES

Domain Name Service:	❑ NO	❑ YES	$ _____
Set Up Fee:	❑ NO	❑ YES	$ _____
Monthly Fee:	❑ NO	❑ YES	$ _____
Yearly Fee:	❑ NO	❑ YES	$ _____

How many user ID's do you get with a domain name? _____

What is the cost of each additional user name? $ _____

How is it charged? Monthly ❑

Yearly ❑

Other ❑

Questions for Internet Service Providers

COMMUNICATION TO PROVIDER

How many modems do they have? _____

What percentage of the time are they all full (i.e., busy signal if you try to connect)? _____

What speed of dial up modems do they support?
    9600 ❏
    14,400 ❏
    28,800 ❏

Additional cost for higher speed modems? ❏ NO ❏ YES $ _____

Same phone # of all speeds of modems? ❏ NO ❏ YES

Do they support 56Kbs connection? ❏ NO ❏ YES $ _____

800# phone access? ❏ NO ❏ YES $ _____

WEB PAGE SERVICES

Do they offer Web services (i.e., the ability to store and allow access to a custom Home Page)? ❏ NO ❏ YES

Initial set up fee? ❏ NO ❏ YES $ _____

Monthly fee? ❏ NO ❏ YES $ _____

Yearly fee? ❏ NO ❏ YES $ _____

Access fee (i.e., number of times the page is accessed)? ❏ NO ❏ YES $ _____

Space usage fee (i.e., a fee based on the amount of disk space used)? ❏ NO ❏ YES $ _____

Do they promote the availability and announcement of the Home Page (i.e., through the available Home Page libraries on the Internet)? ❏ NO ❏ YES $ _____

Do they provide reports as to how many people have accessed your Home Page? ❏ NO ❏ YES $ _____

Questions for Internet Service Providers

WEB PAGE SERVICES (cont.)

How often do they report this information?	Daily ❑ Weekly ❑ Monthly ❑ User Accessible ❑	
Do they offer Web Page creation and management services?	❑ NO ❑ YES	$ _____
Can they provide Web Page links to applications and/or databases?	❑ NO ❑ YES	$ _____
Can they provide credit card processing services?	❑ NO ❑ YES	$ _____

E-MAIL SERVICES

Do they provide automatic reply e-mail boxes?	❑ NO ❑ YES	$ _____

GENERAL

Do they screen USEnet News Groups?	❑ NO ❑ YES
Do they provide complete access to the Internet, or do they block/screen something?	❑ NO ❑ YES
Do they recommend any particular software package(s) for you (i.e., the client software)?	❑ NO ❑ YES
Do they provide instruction on how to set up the user software?	❑ NO ❑ YES
Do they provide documentation for set up of user software?	❑ NO ❑ YES

Questions for Internet Service Providers

GENERAL (cont.)

Do they provide hotline telephone support? ❏ NO ❏ YES

What hours of the day does the hotline operate? ❏ NO ❏ YES

How many hotline support personnel do they have working the phones? _____

How many customers do they have in total? _____

How long have they been a service provider? _____

Do they have tutorials, classes, and/or seminars for new users? ❏ NO ❏ YES

How much do they cost? $ _____

Appendix 7

A More Detailed Analysis

If you believe that a more detailed analysis is required before proceeding in whatever direction or level you choose, then you have two options:

1. **Do it in-house.** Educate yourself or an employee on the subject through seminars, reading, and personal experimentation on the Internet. Get yourself one of the personal Internet access software packages from your local computer store and play with it for a month or two. At the same time, read everything you can about the Internet. Visit your bookstore and buy a few personal computer industry magazines for a couple of months.

2. **Get a consultant.** If, for example, you believe you should allow access to all of your employees through your existing Local Area Network, then you should probably get a consultant to help you review what you have now

More Detailed Analysis

and your options. A consultant will usually be able to actually do the work as well (obviously, for a fee). Again, like the other services involved with the Internet, you should shop for a good consultant.

The author of this book operates a small consulting operation, Business Architects, Inc. This is but one of literally hundreds, if not thousands of groups that can provide the expertise required to review and move your operation forward onto the Internet.

Appendix G

An Example

As president of a small technology import distributor in the U.S., I felt the media hype and pressure to be on the Internet. I asked my employees if anyone knew anything about the Internet. They all responded "yes," and thought we should be on it. No one knew anything beyond that, but they were all insistent and excited about our company being "on it."

In response to this situation, I rushed out to the local computer store and got the least expensive software package that was available (about $20) for connecting to the Internet. After spending a few hours trying to get the package installed and connected to the default service provider, I gave up for the day. The software made the assumption that I had taken the time to read all of the manuals, and that I knew something about the Internet already.

A week or so later, I was back at the computer store exchanging the $20 package for the next package (about $30). Back in the office, I got the same type of results.

Another week or so goes by and I was back at the computer store, this time getting the next available package (about $50). You guessed it. Same results.

An Example

By this time I was getting very frustrated. I returned the package and got a complete refund. While in the computer store, I asked a few people their opinions (which got varying answers), and I bought some computer magazines that had Internet articles in them.

During the next week or two I also visited the bookstore and looked through the 200+ books available on the subject. I selected a few that claimed to be business-oriented.

The magazines were somewhat helpful, but the books turned out to be almost useless. The books got technical fairly quickly, or they gave example after example of what other companies (100 times the size of mine) were doing and what great success they had achieved. The other book turned out to be a thinly disguised get-rich-quick scheme.

Everything I looked at assumed that I already knew some of the fundamentals, or that I had time to sit down for hours on end and learn the fundamentals the hard way. Nowhere could I find the answer to three questions:

1. What is the Internet capable of doing?

2. What areas of my business apply to those Internet capabilities?

3. What are the costs and the paybacks?

At about this time, the surprise came in the mail. I received my credit card bill with charges from three different Internet Service Providers. All included set-up and monthly charges, and a couple had access time charges as well. Total bill was about $300 for these services that I didn't know I had received!

I called each of the providers and, after some explanation, research, and a little arm-twisting, they all agreed to credit my account and cancel the services.

No harm, no foul. Right? I didn't think so. By this time I had seen enough about a package called Internet In A Box from Spry, Inc. It

An Example

was the most expensive package in the computer store (about $140), which is why I had not bought it in the first place.

I bought the package, and after a painless 10 minute installation, I was on the Internet. I was informed during the installation that my charges would be about $9 a month and $9 an hour. That seemed fine, since I didn't know better, and especially since, within 5 minutes after the installation, I was on the Internet in full color graphics and I had not read any of the documentation. It was a very nice package to use, and I was shocked that inside of 30 minutes of Internet browsing, I was browsing some information on a computer in Sweden from my home office in Dallas. I was impressed.

At this point I felt I had the software and the provider I wanted. Now, what to do with it?

The parent company of my company's U.S. operation is located overseas. We must communicate daily by voice, fax, and software exchanges. We spend $1.20 per minute on phone calls and outrageous costs for shipments and overnight deliveries. To try and cut the overnight package costs, we set up a computer overseas with a phone line and modem. We, in the U.S., would dial their computer with our computer and do file transfers. This cut the overnight package costs, but we were now spending $1.20 per minute to transfer files instead of overnight charges.

At my recommendation, our parent company immediately got connected to the Internet. Within one day, we were now able to send files electronically at $9 per hour instead of $1.20 per minute. A one hour file transfer was now $9 instead of $72 per hour (60 minutes x $1.20 per minute). This, alone, paid for the Internet access.

About two months later, we found ourselves spending $250 per month on access time. This got me wondering about what differences there are in Internet access providers' pricing. A little bit of shopping quickly revealed that we could get a local provider for about $20 per month with no hourly access fees. Consequently, we switched service providers.

An Example

When we switched, we realized that we had to keep the old one as well, since we had already published our Internet address to customers and prospects. We did not get a domain name, so when we switched access providers, our e-mail address changed. So, now we pay $9 per month for the old provider so we can check our e-mail (until we get our new address published and known), and $20 per month to the new provider with no hourly fee.

At the time of this book's preparation, we are building our own Home Page. Our marketing person has spent a great deal of time getting our marketing materials presentable with graphics and text, all using Microsoft Windows based software. We gave her a book on Web Page creation, and within two days she was quickly converting our existing marketing materials into Web Page format. The process is not very complex for anyone who works with PC-based text formatting tools already.

We don't see the justification for our own server. In fact, we are not 100% convinced that getting a Web Page is going to result in more business. We shopped for a service provider that will give us Web space for about $500 per year, which is a reasonable price to pay to find out.

Glossary

Baud/bps The terms used to quantify the speed at which a modem allows one computer to communicate with another over a standard telephone line.

Client A computer system that operates in synchronized conjunction with a "server" computer. The client computer typically makes a request of the server, to which the server then performs some operation(s) and returns a result. The client computer is typically smaller in both capacity and power than the server and is generally used to interact with the user, submit a request to the server, and present the server-returned results to the user.

DOS A computer operating system providing the interface between the user and the actual computer hardware.

Terminology & Definitions Reference

E-Mail
A facility on the Internet which allows those connected to send electronic mail messages, documents, files, etc. Each user has a unique address from which mail can be sent and/or received.

File Transfer Protocol (FTP)
A facility on the Internet which allows those connected to view and retrieve information in the form of documents and files.

Gopher
A facility on the Internet which allows those connected to search, view, and retrieve information in the form of documents and files. Similar to the FTP facility with the addition of a variety of advanced searching tools.

GUI
Graphical User Interface. Pronounced "Goo-ee." Examples include Windows, Apple Macintosh.

Home Page
A document created in Hypertext Markup Language format (HTML) for use on the World Wide Web(WWW).

Kbps
The term used to quantify the speed at which a modem allows one computer to communicate with another over a standard telephone line, measured in thousands. ("K" meaning kilo; kilo bits per second)

Macintosh
Apple computer and operating environment that allows the user to interact with the computer in a graphical enviroment. Not "IBM PC Compatible."

Mega Byte (MB)
The term used to quantify the capacity of a computer in terms of both memory and disk storage.

Terminology & Definitions Reference

Modem A peripheral hardware device for a computer used to make a connection to other computer(s) over standard telephone lines.

Mosaic A software program which allows the Internet connected user to browse the World Wide Web.

Mouse The computer peripheral device used to interact with a graphical display and application.

NCSA National Computer Science Administration. The federal organization which manages the non-commercial, education-oriented usage of the Internet.

NetScape A software program which allows the Internet connected user to browse the World Wide Web.

OS/2 A computer operating system providing the interface between the user and the actual computer hardware.

Router A computer hardware device which dynamically manages the flow of information to and from computers connected to the Internet.

Server A computer system that operates in synchronized conjunction with a "client" computer. The client computer typically makes a request of the server, to which the server then performs some operation(s) and returns a result. The server computer is typically larger in both capacity and power than the client and is generally used to store large volumes of information.

Terminology & Definitions Reference

Service Provider A company that provides connection services into the Internet for end-users and/or other companies.

SVGA A standard type of display connected to a personal computer which allows for high resolution graphics. This type of display provides greater graphical abilities than a VGA ("S" meaning "Super" VGA)

Unix A computer operating system providing the interface between the user and the actual computer hardware.

VGA A standard type of display connected to a personal computer which allows for high resolution graphics.

Windows Microsoft computer operating environment which allows the user to interact with the computer in a graphical environment. Used in "IBM PC Compatible" personal computers.

World Wide Web
WWW
Web A facility on the Internet which allows those connected to view interconnected documents comprised of text and graphics. WWW documents are stored in Hypertext Markup Language (HTML). WWW documents are commonly referred to as Home Pages.

Index

A

address, internet, 16-17, 27, 96-97
advertising, 13, 37, 43-44, 46, 83, 100
America On-Line, 8, 9
audio, 44
authors, 16

B

broadcasting/media, 21, 107
brochures, 42, 48
business applications, 12-13, 15-16, 29, 36, 78
business communications, 53
business operations, 19, 29

C

catalogs, 14, 48
client, 86, 102
communication, external, 14, 31-34
communication, internal, 13-14
competition, 69-70
CompuServe, 8, 9
construction, 21-22
consultants, 84
cost justification, 4, 31-32, 49, 59-60, 109-110
credit cards, 73
customer, business, 35-36
customer, communication from, 33-34, 73
customer, communication to, 31-33, 69-70
customer, individual, 36-38
customer, international, 34-35
customer feedback, 27, 33-34

D

discussion/news groups, 20-21, 27, 87
display, 45, 82
domain name, 96-97, 101, 110

Index

E

education, 21, 22
electronic mail (e-mail), 13, 16, 18, 29, 36, 41, 44-45, 54, 59 60, 63, 65-66, 73, 86, 95, 103, 110
end-user access, 91-92

F

fax, 31-34, 50, 55, 109
file transfer protocol (FTP), 87, 95
firewall, 72
flame, 5, 10
foreign interest, 23
forms, 13, 28, 31, 34, 46, 48-50
future, 75

G

general business, 19-20, 22
gopher, 112
government, 6, 15, 23, 75
graphics, 44-45, 48-49
growth, 9, 28

H

hardware, 62, 65-66, 81-84
history, internet, 6
home page, 16, 18, 46-47, 50, 54, 59, 73, 88, 95, 102, 110

I

Information Superhighway, 3, 5-6
international, 20, 34-35, 59-60
internet access/service provider, 2, 11, 16, 63, 82, 86, 92, 99-104, 109
internet applications, 12-13, 16, 36, 86
internet server, 62, 64-65, 72, 81, 83, 85, 88-93
internet server software, 64
internet user software, 85-88
ISDN, 92-93

L

law, 24, 60
levels of access, 65-66
local area network (LAN), 36, 66, 84, 89

M

Macintosh, 62, 82, 88
magazines, 15-16, 71, 87, 100, 105, 108
mail, 5-7, 10, 13, 15-16, 18, 95, 108
mailings, 11, 44, 47-48, 50, 100
marketing, 1, 4, 14, 17, 20, 33, 36-37, 43-44, 46, 50, 54, 78, 88, 100, 110
material goods, 15
Microsoft, 9, 47, 66

Index

Microsoft Windows, 47, 82, 87, 89, 110
modem, 62, 65-66, 82, 84, 86, 91-93, 102, 109
monitor (see display)
mouse, 83, 86

N

National Science Foundation (NSF), 6
netiquette, 9, 44, 48
NetScape, 113
newsletters, 32

O

OS/2, 82, 88
overnight delivery, 32, 34, 36, 59, 109

P

physical goods, 31, 40
press release, 50-51
Prodigy, 8, 9
product delivery, 14
product support, 40-41, 50
publications, 15

R

retail, 22, 24
router, 84, 89, 96

S

sales, 20, 31, 35-36, 40, 43, 53-55
sales support, 55
security, employees, 73-75
security, information, 71-72
security, transactions, 72-73, 75
services industry, 24
soft products, 39-40, 60
software, 62-63, 64, 65-66, 85-90
stock market, 25-26
Sun, 83
suppliers, 14, 20, 57
support, 8-9, 33, 40-41, 55, 70, 90, 102, 104
SVGA, 82

T

taxes, 23, 26
technology, 4, 7, 10, 14, 28, 61-62, 66-67, 70, 74, 81, 85, 92, 97

U

Unix, 7, 82-83, 86, 89
usage, 10, 12, 17, 29, 31, 36, 41, 50, 61, 63-64, 67, 71, 74, 102

Index

V

VGA, 82
video, 8, 44

W

warranty, 40-41, 50
web browser, 86-87
web page (see also home page),
 101-102, 110, 112
Windows (see Microsoft
 Windows)
World Wide Web (Web, WWW),
 44, 82, 86-88, 95, 101-103, 110, 112

Best-Selling Small Business Books
Available at your local bookstore!

"The writers of the Small Business Sourcebooks series all have that practical, 'we've done it and it works' approach that is so important to the entrepreneur or owner of a growing business."
—Bob Newzell, Host/Producer, "Sales Talk" on the Business Radio Network

Mancuso's Small Business Basics by Joseph R. Mancuso
Mancuso's expertise will guide you through choosing your business venture, raising capital, and selecting business partners, lawyers, and accountants. Also, learn how to manage for short and long-term growth and handle government requirements.
188 pages, ISBN 1-57071-076-7 (paperback)

Your First Business Plan by Joseph Covello and Brian Hazelgren
"In easy-to-follow chapters the authors simplify the process of writing a plan by using an uncomplicated question-and-answer style."
—Starred Review in *Library Journal*
152 pages, ISBN 1-57071-044-9 (paperback), $9.95

The Small Business Legal Guide by Lynne Ann Frasier, Esq.
"...the definitive 'how to' business start-up book."
—Ken Blanchard, Co-author, "The One-Minute Manager"
Essential information on incorporating, partnerships, trademarks, understanding and negotiating contracts, patents, hiring employees and independent contractors, and franchising. Includes forms and agreements you can use.
176 pages, ISBN 1-57071-060-0 (paperback)

Great Idea! Now What? by Howard Bronson and Peter Lange
Turn your idea, invention or business concept into a moneymaking success with a complete process for developing, testing, producing and marketing your great idea.
"One of the best how-to marketing books ever written!"
—CNBC, *Smart Money*
224 pages, ISBN 1-57071-039-2 (paperback), $9.95

Real World Customer Service by Bernice B. Johnston
Give your business the tools to please even the toughest customers and make them yours for life. With complete processes and scripts you can use, this book is devoted to the actual handling of customer complaints for front-line employees.
144 pages, ISBN 1-57071-062-7 (paperback)

The Small Business Survival Guide by Robert E. Fleury
"Innovative ways of managing cash flow and accounting problems."
—Jane Applegate, Syndicated Columnist, *Los Angeles Times*
"One of the 75 best resources for starting a company."
—*Inc. Magazine*
256 pages, ISBN 1-57071-045-2 (paperback), $17.95

The Complete Book of Business Plans by Joseph Covello and Brian Hazelgren
With 11 actual plans to guide you, this book will show you how to write a powerful and effective business plan. Eliminate the frustration of starting a new business by learning the critical elements required by investors, lenders, and buyers.
328 pages, ISBN 0-942061-41-1 (paperback), $19.95

Grow Your Business With
America's #1 Small Business Series

"If I had these books when I first started in business I wouldn't have had to learn the hard way."
—*Vera Gold, Radio Talk Show Host and Founder of the Money Radio Business Format*

The Small Business Start-Up Guide by Hal Root and Steve Koenig
Learn how to incorporate, find investors, handle legal and governmental restrictions, and raise capital. Includes complete forms and individual state requirements.
152 pages, ISBN 0-942061-70-5 (hardcover) • ISBN 0-942061-67-5 (paperback)

Smart Hiring by Robert W. Wendover
Everything you need to know to find and hire the right employee. Learn the critical aspects of recruiting, evaluating applications and resumes, and interviewing. Includes 500 great interview questions your business should use.
152 pages, ISBN 0-942061-56-X (paperback)

Getting Paid In Full by W. Kelsea Wilber
Collect the money you are owed and develop a system to train customers to pay on time. Includes sample collection letters and credit applications that bring results!
144 pages, ISBN 0-942061-71-3 (hardcover) • ISBN 0-942061-68-3 (paperback)

How to Sharpen Your Competitive Edge by Don Reynolds, Jr.
Discover the keys to successfully positioning your business and edging out the competition. Use your current resources to develop your competitive edge!
200 pages, ISBN 0-942061-73-X (hardcover) • ISBN 0-942061-72-1 (paperback)

Protect Your Business by Sgt. James Nelson and Ofc. Terry Davis
Safeguard your business against shoplifting, employee theft, and more. Includes instructions for evaluating security devices and purchasing alarm equipment.
144 pages, ISBN 0-942061-66-7 (paperback)

How to Market Your Business by Ian B. Rosengarten, MS, MPH
An A-Z guide to the tools and tactics for marketing your business, including public service announcements, TV and radio ads, telemarketing, and more.
152 pages, ISBN 0-942061-48-9 (hardcover) • ISBN 0-942061-45-4 (paperback)

How to Get a Loan or Line of Credit by Bryan E. Milling
Discover how bankers review loan requests and find out how to increase your chances of getting a loan. Includes step-by-step financial forms and SBA loan facts.
152 pages, ISBN 0-942061-46-2 (hardcover) • ISBN 0-942061-43-8 (paperback)

To order these books or any other of our many publications, *please contact your local bookseller* or call Sourcebooks at 708-961-3900. Get a copy of our catalog by writing or faxing:

Sourcebooks, Inc.
P. O. Box 372
Naperville, IL 60566
(708) 961-3900
FAX: (708) 961-2168
Thank you for your interest!